English Articles and Determiners

Up Close

Also by Mark Lester

Practice Makes Perfect: English Verb Tenses Up Close

Practice Makes Perfect: Advanced English Grammar for ESL Learners

The Big Book of English Verbs

McGraw-Hill's Essential ESL Grammar

McGraw-Hill's Essential English Irregular Verbs

English Grammar Drills

The McGraw-Hill Handbook of English Grammar and Usage (with Larry Beason)

English Articles and Determiners

Up Close

Mark Lester, PhD

New York Chicago San Francisco Athens London Madrid
Mexico City Milan New Delhi Singapore Sydney Toronto

1 2 3 4 5 6 7 8 9 10 11 12 13 14 15 16 17 18   QFR/QFR   1 0 9 8 7 6 5 4 3

ISBN   978-0-07-175206-0
MHID   0-07-175206-4

e-ISBN   978-0-07-175355-5
e-MHID   0-07-175355-9

Library of Congress Control Number   2013930333

McGraw-Hill Education, the McGraw-Hill Education logo, Practice Makes Perfect, and related trade dress are trademarks or registered trademarks of McGraw-Hill Education and/or its affiliates in the United States and other countries and may not be used without written permission. All other trademarks are the property of their respective owners. McGraw-Hill Education is not associated with any product or vendor mentioned in this book.

Interior design by Village Typographers, Inc.

McGraw-Hill Education products are available at special quantity discounts to use as premiums and sales promotions or for use in corporate training programs. To contact a representative, please visit the Contact Us pages at www.mhprofessional.com.

This book is printed on acid-free paper.

Contents

II DETERMINERS

Preface

This book focuses on the meaning and use of a large and important class of pre-adjective noun modifiers: articles and determiners. This book is unique in that it deals only with this one special group of noun modifiers. Consequently, it is able to provide a much greater in-depth treatment than would be possible in a more conventional grammar book that also covers a hundred other topics. While many of the topics and issues covered will be familiar to you, the depth and detail of the coverage will address many issues that will be totally new to you.

This book is intended for advanced English learners. It assumes that you are comfortable with a college-level English vocabulary. The grammatical vocabulary, however, is quite ordinary. The terms used in this book are ones that you have been using since high school.

The book contains a number of short exercises, all with answers provided in the Answer key. The purpose of the exercises is for you to test your own understanding of a concept or to practice a particular skill or technique. These exercises are important as a way for you to ensure that what you have studied has really been learned. It is all too easy to have a passive understanding of the material without realizing that you are dependent on the support provided by the instruction material.

This book has two goals, one obvious and one not so obvious. The first and most obvious goal is to help you use articles and determiners correctly. Articles and determiners are some of the most difficult words for nonnative speakers to use correctly. Since they are also some of the most frequently used words in English, the opportunity for nonnative speakers to make mistakes with them is nearly unlimited.

A substantial portion of the text is devoted to a second goal: helping you understand the sometimes quite subtle implications in the way native speakers use articles and determiners, especially in informal, conversational settings. Accordingly, much of the book deals with issues of usage—exploring the consequences of different stylistic choices in the ways we use articles and determiners.

There are two main components. Part I deals with each category of article in turn. Historically, grammar books recognized only two articles: the indefinite article *a/an* and the definite article *the*. However, we will add two additional articles: *some/any* (which we will treat as a unit) and the zero article, ∅. (A zero article is the option of choosing to have no overt article where one would normally be expected. Here is a sentence with two zero articles: ∅ *Onions give me* ∅ *indigestion.*)

Part II deals with determiners, which are a large and heterogeneous group of pre-adjective noun modifiers that "determine" which noun is being talked about. There are two main types of determiners: definite determiners and quantifiers. Definite determiners serve to define or specify the noun modified by the determiners. Here are some examples of definite determiners:

Demonstrative determiners: *this, that, these, those*
Possessive determiners: *my, our, your, his, her, its, their*

Quantifiers are determiners that specify the quantity or amount of the noun being modified. Here are some typical examples of quantifiers: *all, some, much, many, few, little,* and so on.

Quantifiers account for a disproportionately large number of errors for native and nonnative speakers alike. Quantifiers are extremely sensitive to the distinction between count and noncount nouns, for example we say "many problems" because "problems" is a count noun, but "much confusion" because "confusion" is a noncount noun.

English
Articles and
Determiners
Up Close

ARTICLES

An introduction to articles

This chapter will give you the information you need to use articles correctly and to understand the often subtle ways native speakers use articles to express meaning.

Four types of articles

Traditionally, there are only two articles: the definite article *the* and the indefinite article *a/an*. However, in this presentation (as in most modern grammar books), we recognize no less than a total of *four* different types of articles (i.e., counting *any* as the counterpart of *some* in questions and negative statements and not as a separate article in its own right):

- ◆ the definite article *the*
- ◆ the singular indefinite article *a/an*
- ◆ the indefinite article *some*
- ◆ the zero article, ∅

Here are examples of the four types of articles:

- ◆ the definite article *the*

> I recognized the voices that were coming from inside the house.
> The terms of the agreement have not yet been settled.

- ◆ the singular indefinite article *a/an*

> I noticed a new leak in the patio roof tonight.
> There has been an accident on northbound I-405.

- ◆ the indefinite article *some*

> We bought some maps at a gas station on the way up.
> There is some luggage still on the bus.

◆ the zero article, ∅

 ∅ Luggage must be placed under the seats during the flight.
 ∅ Bananas are high in ∅ potassium.

Using a common noun without any overt article or determiner is referred to as using a zero article. A zero article normally indicates that a noun is being used generically as a generalization about a whole category. In the two previous examples, the use of a zero article in the first example means that the first sentence is talking about all luggage, not any one particular piece of luggage. The use of the zero article in the second example signals that the sentence is making a generalization about the nature of all bananas.

Identifying the four articles *Underline each of the articles in the following sentences, and then indicate which of the four types it is: definite article (def.); singular indefinite article (sing. indef.); indefinite article* some *(indef. some) or zero article (zero). An example is provided.*

Note: In questions and negative statements some *automatically changes to* any. *For example, compare the following sentences:*

I have some *money.*

Question: Do you have *any* money?

Negative: I don't have *any* money.

We will treat these uses of any *as obligatory alternative forms of the indefinite article* some.

zero   def.   indef. *some*

∅ Required courses are offered in <u>the</u> morning and on <u>some</u> afternoons.

1. Family names come from all over the world.

2. An interest payment will be due on the first of the month.

3. What they did really took some courage.

4. Players have to enter the stadium though a special gate.

5. Some costs cannot be passed on to customers and must be absorbed by the company.

6. Experience is a stern and unforgiving teacher.

7. They inherited property on the coast from a distant relative.

8. The police were not able to find any solid evidence connecting the initial suspects to the crime.

9. Technically, glass is not a solid, because it does not have a rigid structure.

10. Some fish is very high in omega-3 fatty acid.

Categories of nouns

The main presentation in Part I is in four chapters, one chapter for each of the four types of article:

1. Definite article *the*

2. Singular indefinite article *a/an*

3. Indefinite article *some*

4. Zero article, ∅

However, before we look at the four different types of articles in detail in the following sections, we need to understand the complicated interrelation between the type of article and the different grammatical categories of nouns that these articles modify. These grammatical categories determine which articles are available for us to choose from. Failure to correctly identify the grammatical category of the noun that an article modifies is a common source of error in selecting the proper article.

There are three different categories of nouns: (1) singular count nouns (count nouns used in the singular form), (2) plural count nouns (count nouns used in the plural form), and (3) noncount nouns (nouns that cannot be counted or used in the plural form).

Apple, for example, is a typical count noun. It can be used both in the singular and plural forms:

SINGULAR: I usually pack an <u>apple</u> in my lunch.
PLURAL: Take some <u>apples</u> with you.

Fruit is a typical noncount noun that cannot be counted or used in the plural:

X one <u>fruit</u>,   **X** two <u>fruits</u>,   **X** a dozen <u>fruits</u>

Note: The symbol **X** is used throughout the book to indicate that the following word, phrase, or sentence is ungrammatical.

The following chart shows which articles can be used with which categories of nouns:

CATEGORIES OF NOUN THAT ARTICLE IS USED WITH

TYPES OF ARTICLE	SING. COUNT	PL. COUNT	NONCOUNT
Def. *the*	Yes	Yes	*
Sing. indef. *a/an*	Yes	No	No
Indef. *some*	No	Yes	Yes
Zero, ∅	No	Yes	Yes

* When used generically, noncount nouns do not normally use *the*, but when used nongenerically, *the* is often used.

GENERIC:	Many people are allergic to ∅ milk.
NONGENERIC:	The milk is on the table.

The distinction between generic and nongeneric uses of noncount nouns will be discussed in detail in "Distinguishing between count and noncount nouns."

The following are examples of each type of article with all of the noun categories that it can be used with grammatically. (The articles are in bold. The nouns being modified are underlined.)

Definite article *the*

SINGULAR COUNT NOUN:	**The** bird feeder is empty again.
PLURAL COUNT NOUN:	Would you repeat **the** directions?
NONCOUNT NOUN:	**The** confusion was understandable.

Singular article *a/an*

SINGULAR COUNT NOUN:	I am going to be away at **a** conference next week.
	Move it **an** inch to the left.

Plural article *some*

PLURAL COUNT NOUN:	Here are **some** forms that you need to fill out.
NONCOUNT NOUN:	Would you like **some** coffee?

Zero article, ∅

PLURAL COUNT NOUN:	∅ Budgets are always revised.
NONCOUNT NOUN:	∅ Necessity is the mother of ∅ invention. (saying)

Connecting article types with noun categories *All of the articles in the following sentences are correctly used. First, underline each article, and identify which of the four article types it belongs to. Second, underline twice the noun each article modifies, and identify which of the three noun categories the modified noun belongs to. (Remember, you will have to add the zero article to the sentence if it is called for.) An example is provided.*

Zero   pl. count   def. pl. count   indef. *some* pl. count

Ø Required <u>courses</u> are offered in <u>the</u> <u>mornings</u> and on <u>some</u> <u>afternoons</u>.

1. I made a big mistake right at the beginning.

2. We are really trying to cut back on salt.

3. Some versions of the story have a totally different outcome.

4. Big projects always tend to run out of time.

5. The team has shown some signs of improvement lately.

6. We got a loan to make some repairs.

7. He deals with the integration of different computer systems.

8. The failures came as a complete surprise.

9. People are too busy these days.

10. The university offers a number of scholarships.

Singular count nouns, plural count nouns, and noncount nouns

The remainder of this introductory chapter discusses the categories of nouns that articles modify: singular count nouns, plural count nouns, and noncount nouns. The main focus will be on noncount nouns, which are a major source of errors for nonnative speakers. It is important to keep in mind this discussion of the categories of nouns, because it will not be repeated in the following chapters that deal with each of the four types of articles or in Part II, which deals with determiners.

Singular count nouns and plural count nouns are intimately connected. The main characteristic of a normal count noun is that we can use it with *both* singular *and* plural forms. Of course, English being English, a few exceptional count nouns do not have both singular and plural forms. A few singular count nouns ending in *-s* have no corresponding plural (e.g., *news, politics, statistics*). In other words, these nouns are inherently singular without any possibility of a plural form or a plural meaning.

> The <u>news</u> is good tonight.
> The <u>news</u> **X** are good tonight.

Thirty-some plural count nouns do not have singular count noun counterparts (e.g., *people, police, scissors, pants, savings, wages*).

> The <u>people</u> who couldn't get tickets were very upset.
> The <u>people</u> who couldn't get tickets **X** is very upset.

Some of these plural-only nouns have regular count noun counterparts, but of course, they do not mean the same thing. For example, the plural-only noun *savings* means the total amount of money a person has put aside:

> My parents have invested their <u>savings</u> only in government bonds.

The count noun meaning of *savings* is the particular amount of money that someone earned in a specific transaction:

> I got a <u>savings</u> of $15 by getting the coat online.

The remaining 99.99% of count nouns have both singular and plural forms.

There is no requirement that count nouns form their plurals in a regular way. The only requirement is that count nouns have plural meanings as well as singular meanings. For example, the noun *deer* is highly irregular in that it has no recognizable plural form at all:

> SINGULAR: We saw a <u>deer</u> in our backyard last night.
> PLURAL: We saw three <u>deer</u> in our backyard last night.

Nevertheless, *deer* clearly has a singular meaning in the first sentence as we can tell from the use of the singular article *a. Deer* is plural in the second sentence as we can tell from the use of the plural number word *three*.

In grammatical terms, the definition of count nouns is that they can be counted. In other words, for a noun to be a count noun, the noun must be freely countable with the cardinal number words *one, two, three, four*, and so on:

> <u>one</u> apple, <u>two</u> apples, <u>three</u> apples, <u>four</u> apples . . .
> <u>one</u> idea, <u>two</u> ideas, <u>three</u> ideas, <u>four</u> ideas . . .

Noncount nouns are a totally different story. As the name tells us, noncount nouns cannot be counted with any cardinal number words, singular or plural. For example, here are two noncount nouns: *smog* and *health*. When we try to use the same cardinal number words we used earlier with the count nouns *apple* and *idea*, the results are uniformly ungrammatical:

> **X** one smog, **X** two smogs, **X** three smogs, **X** four smogs
> **X** one health, **X** two healths, **X** three healths, **X** four healths

The easiest quick test to see if a noun is a count noun or a noncount noun is to see if the noun can be used in the plural (remember, we are talking about meaning, not form):

> **Count noun:** If you can grammatically use a noun in its plural form in a sentence, then the noun is countable.
> **Noncount noun:** If you cannot grammatically use a noun in its plural form in a sentence, then the noun is noncountable.

Here are some examples of applying this test to a few sample words:

1. *risk*: The risks associated with the plan are unacceptably high.
   Answer: Grammatical, so risk is a countable noun.

2. *silence*: We love the **X** silences when we get out of the city.
   Answer: Ungrammatical, so silence is a noncount noun.

3. *implication*: There are a lot of implications that we haven't explored.
   Answer: Grammatical, so implication is a count noun.

4. *integration*: The **X** integrations of American schools was a huge issue.
   Answer: Ungrammatical, so integration is a noncount noun.

There is one important exception to the general rule that noncount nouns cannot be used in the plural. Sometimes noncount nouns can be used in the plural form *but only if the plural form does not have a plural meaning*. Instead, the plural form has a completely unrelated meaning: "different kinds of." Here are some examples that pair together two different uses of the same noncount noun: first with the normal noncount meaning (which is ungrammatical in the plural), and second with the meaning of "different kinds of" (which is grammatical in the plural form).

> **cheese**
> NORMAL NONCOUNT MEANING: We need to get more cheese.
>   **X** We need to get more cheeses.
> "DIFFERENT KINDS OF" MEANING: The store carries hundreds of cheeses.

Note: Cheeses is actually a plural noun, as we can see when we make it the subject of a sentence and have a plural verb agree with it: These cheeses are really good.

Spanish

NORMAL NONCOUNT MEANING:	Thomas is taking <u>Spanish</u> this fall.
	X Thomas is taking <u>Spanishes</u> this fall.
"DIFFERENT KINDS OF" MEANING:	There are several <u>Spanishes</u> spoken in Latin America.

taste

NORMAL NONCOUNT MEANING:	She has good <u>taste</u>.
	X She has good <u>tastes</u>.
"DIFFERENT KINDS OF" MEANING:	There is no accounting for <u>tastes</u>.

experience

NORMAL NONCOUNT MEANING:	<u>Experience</u> is the best teacher. (saying)
	X <u>Experiences</u> are the best teachers.
"DIFFERENT KINDS OF" MEANING:	Travel gives us a wide range of <u>experiences</u>.

From this point on in our discussion, we will set aside the special use of noncount nouns in the meaning of "different kinds of."

Distinguishing between count and noncount nouns

The remainder of this section is devoted to giving you some practical ways to distinguish between count and noncount nouns.

The distinction between count and noncount nouns is widespread in languages around the world. In very broad terms, it is a semantic distinction between nouns that refer to things and ideas considered as individual entities (count nouns) as opposed to things and ideas that we think of as indivisible whole entities or categories (noncount nouns), not as individual entities.

Here is a simple example that exemplifies the difference between viewing nouns as referring to individual objects and viewing nouns as referring to undifferentiated masses:

| COUNT NOUN: | cloud |
| NONCOUNT NOUN: | fog |

Cloud and *fog* are physically exactly the some thing: visible water vapor. The difference is in our perception of them. We perceive a cloud as an individual object. We perceive fog as an undifferentiated mass. Accordingly, we treat *cloud* as a count noun and *fog* as a noncount noun.

There were several <u>clouds</u> on the horizon.
There was <u>fog</u> on the horizon.

As we would expect, we cannot pluralize the noncount noun *fog*:

X There were <u>fogs</u> on the horizon.

It is convenient to divide noncount nouns into two groups: **concrete** and **abstract**. Concrete noncount nouns refer to concrete, physical objects that you can touch or perceive, for example, *cheese, cement, dust, paper, rain, cotton,* and *milk*. Abstract noncount nouns refer to abstractions and other intangible things and ideas, for example, *charity, smiling, Spanish, electricity, tennis,* and *knowledge*.

The group of concrete nouns is smaller than the group of abstract nouns and, not surprisingly, much easier to talk about. Accordingly, we will begin with a discussion of concrete nouns.

Concrete noncount nouns

Many concrete noncount nouns fall into the following four semantic categories:

1. Mass nouns

2. Liquids and gases (both clear and with suspended solids)

3. Categories of raw or basic materials

4. Categorical terms for classes of similar objects

Mass nouns

Many concrete noncount nouns like *dust, rice,* or *hair* refer to objects that occur in small particles or pieces that we consider collectively in the aggregate as opposed to larger objects that we consider as individuals. We typically refer to these smaller objects collectively or as a group or mass.

> The furniture was covered in dust.
> I cooked the rice for 20 minutes.
> The carpet always shows dog hair.

For this reason, we will refer to this semantic group of noncount nouns as **mass nouns**. Note: The term *mass noun* is also sometimes used more broadly as a synonym for *count noun*. In this book, however, we will use the term *mass noun* narrowly as a label for this one particular semantic category of concrete noncount nouns.

An obvious question that arises is how small do objects have to be for them to be considered mass nouns? The following exercise may help you answer this question for yourself.

The difference in size between count nouns and noncount mass nouns *The following list of nouns refers to small objects. Some are count nouns and some are noncount mass nouns. Indicate whether you think the noun is a count noun or a noncount mass noun. The first question is done as an example.*

	COUNT	NONCOUNT MASS
seed	X	
1. powder		
2. pebble		
3. fur		
4. pea		
5. rock		
6. grit		
7. nut		
8. sand		
9. grain		
10. stone		

How would you characterize in a few words what the difference is in size between count nouns and noncount mass nouns? Check the answer in the Answer key, and see if you agree.

There is a big difference between the way we talk about concrete count nouns and the way we talk about concrete noncount mass nouns. For example, contrast the differences between the way we talk about the count noun *tree* and the concrete noncount mass noun *grass*. We use the count noun *tree* to talk about a specific individual tree or some specific group of trees.

A <u>tree</u> fell across the road and temporarily blocked it.
The <u>tree</u> on the patio really helps keep the house cool.
Those <u>trees</u> shelter the house against the wind.
The nursery is going to deliver the two new <u>trees</u> we bought.

The noncount mass noun *grass*, on the other hand, refers to a class of objects that we can talk about only collectively as an undifferentiated whole group:

> We planted grass in the front yard.
> The grass isn't getting enough water.
> The lawnmower is cutting the grass too short.

When we try to talk about *grass* as an individual object, the results are totally ungrammatical:

> I got a **X** grass in my eye as I was cutting the lawn.
> One **X** grass needs to be replaced.
> The sprinkler is getting those four **X** grasses too wet.
> I am going to weed the two **X** grasses.

Liquids and gases (both clear and with suspended solids)

Liquids and gases are like noncount mass nouns in that they are always treated as indivisible categories. Here are some examples:

> LIQUIDS: blood, coffee, milk, gasoline, soup, syrup
> GASES: air, oxygen, smoke, steam

If we try to use these nouns in the plural, they are ungrammatical.

> LIQUIDS: I cut myself and got some **X** bloods on my new shirt.
> I am totally addicted to **X** coffees.
> People get a lot of their calcium from **X** milks.
> The cost of **X** gasolines fluctuates wildly.
>
> GASES: The **X** airs in the small meeting room were getting stuffy.
> Plants are the main source of **X** oxygens.
> **X** Smokes from the forest fires were blocking out the sun.
> The buildings downtown are heated by **X** steams.

Note: We often use number words with the pluralized names of liquids, but these expressions are contractions of longer expressions in which the noncount nouns are inside prepositional phrases beginning with *of*. The number words are actually modifying the count nouns at the head of the prepositional phrases, not the noncount nouns that are locked up inside the *of* preposition phase. For example, for the sentence,

> We would like four coffees, please.

the full underlying sentence is,

> We would like four **cups** of coffee, please.

The number word *four* actually modifies the understood plural count noun *cups*, not the noncount mass noun *coffee*.

Identifying noncount nouns that are liquids and gases *The underlined nouns in the following sentences are all plural. Some of the plurals are correctly used because the nouns are count nouns. Other plurals are correctly used because the plurals are contracted forms of prepositional phrases containing* of. *The remaining plural forms are ungrammatical because they are noncount nouns used in the plural for names of liquids or gases.*

For each underlined noun, determine first whether the underlined noun is grammatical or ungrammatical. If the noun is grammatical, is it grammatical because it is (a) a count noun or (b) a contracted form containing "of"? Three examples are given.

The <u>drops</u> are added to the eye one at a time.

(a) grammatical because <u>drops</u> is a count noun

The <u>condensations</u> were getting all over the windshield, and we couldn't see.

ungrammatical because <u>condensation</u> is a noncount noun—the name of a liquid

We had some <u>beers</u> with our friends after work.

(b) grammatical because some <u>beers</u> is a contracted form of a prepositional phrase containing of: *some bottles/glasses of beer*

1. The kids were getting <u>honeys</u> all over their hands and faces.

_____

2. If vehicles have full tanks, heat can cause the <u>gases</u> to overflow.

_____

3. <u>Seawaters</u> are corroding all the intake pipes.

_____

4. The <u>streams</u> in this area all flow east.

_____

5. In late summer, there is always <u>heat hazes</u> hanging in the air.

_____

6. I ordered some <u>lemonades</u> for the kids.

_____

7. <u>Eggs</u> are a good source of protein.

_____

8. It was so hot we stopped and had <u>lemonades</u>.

_____

9. The <u>exhausts</u> were leaking back into the truck and making us sick.

_____

10. A common mistake in making pancakes is getting the <u>batters</u> too thick.

_____

Categories of raw or basic materials

This large and diverse category consists of categories of basic or raw materials that specific countable objects are made from. It is convenient to break this category into two groups: physical materials and basic food stuffs:

Physical materials

brick	plastic
cement	sandstone
chalk	steel
concrete	stone
granite	wood

names of all the physical elements (*lead, copper, iron, zinc,* etc.)
names of types of cloth (*cotton, wool, silk, rayon, nylon, polyester,* etc.)

> All the pathways are made of <u>cement</u>.
> The price of <u>copper</u> has gone through the roof.
> I don't wear <u>wool</u>, because it makes my skin itch.

Basic food stuffs

bacon	flour
beef	ham
bread	hamburger
butter	meat
cheese	peanut butter
coffee	pork

> A lot of simple dishes start with <u>ground beef</u>.
> The sauce is made with <u>butter</u>.
> We need to get a couple of pounds of <u>coffee</u>.

As expected, all of these examples of noncount nouns become ungrammatical if they are used in the plural:

> All the pathways are made of **X** cements.
> The price of **X** coppers has gone through the roof.
> I don't wear **X** wools, because they make my skin itch.
> A lot of simple dishes start with **X** ground beefs.
> The sauce is made with **X** butters.
> We need to get a couple of pounds of **X** coffees.

Categorical terms for classes of similar objects

Some concrete noncount nouns refer to entire categories of count nouns that are individual members of a larger class defined by the noncount noun. For example, the noncount noun *clothing* is a categorical term for all the different items that we wear: *shirt, tie, blouse, dress,* and *sweater* (all of which are individual count nouns).

The noncount categorical noun *clothing* cannot be used in the plural:

> **X** Put all your dirty clothings into the basket in the closet.

However, all the individual items of clothing are count nouns and can be made plural:

> I had two shirts, several ties, and one sweater in my closet.

Here are some more examples:

NONCOUNT CATEGORY	COUNTABLE MEMBERS OF THE CATEGORY
luggage	suitcases, handbags, backpacks, trunks
furniture	sofas, couches, chairs, tables, bookcases
mail	postcards, letters, magazines, bills

As we would expect, the noncount-category terms cannot be used in the plural:

> Please put your **X** luggages under your seats.
> We need to put some of the **X** furnitures into storage.
> I have a week's worth of **X** mails to answer.

Noncount categorical terms *The following are groups of semantically related words. Each group contains a mixture of a single noncount categorical term together with several countable nouns that fit into that semantic category. Find the noncount categorical term. Confirm your answer by pluralizing all of the words. The plural of the noncount categorical term will, of course, be ungrammatical. The first question is done as an example.*

ring, bracelet, jewelry, necklace, earring

ring, bracelet, jewelry, necklace, earring

Confirmation: rings, bracelets, X jewelries, necklaces, earrings

1. quarter, dime, dollar, penny, money

   _____

2. fruit, apple, banana, peach, orange

   _____

3. wrapper, scrap, banana peel, trash, carton

   _____

4. car, bus, traffic, truck, motorcycle

   _____

5. silverware, knife, fork, spoon

   _____

6. stapler, computer, copier, printer, equipment

   _____

7. mountain, scenery, lake, waterfall, valley

   _____

8. shoe, boot, sandal, heel, footwear

   _____

9. apartment, flat, house, housing, room

10. fact, opinion, information, note, memo, list

Abstract noncount nouns

The distinction between abstract and concrete nouns is a simple, practical one: abstract nouns refer to intangible things such as ideas and concepts, while concrete nouns refer to tangible things. The same difference we saw between count and noncount concrete nouns also holds between count and noncount abstract nouns: abstract count nouns refer to things and ideas that we perceive as individual, distinct entities. We can compare and contrast these entities, and (more to the immediate point) we can talk about them in the plural.

Abstract noncount nouns are quite different. Abstract noncount nouns refer to things and ideas we perceive as qualities or whole entire conditions or categories. For example, the abstract noncount noun *beauty* refers to the condition or state of being beautiful. We cannot count it or pluralize it as we could a count noun.

Don't think of abstract nouns as always being noncount nouns. Abstract nouns can be either count nouns or noncount nouns. For example, compare the abstract noncount noun *homework* with the abstract count noun *assignment*. *Homework* is a kind of obligation or commitment. We cannot count it or pluralize it. The count noun *assignment* is totally different. It is a specific, definable task. We can talk about this task any way we want. We can compare your assignment with my assignment. We can count the different assignments and pluralize the word.

The group of abstract noncount nouns is much larger and more diverse than the previous group of concrete noncount nouns. The very term *abstract noun* conjures up lists of large, difficult-to-define concepts such as the following:

truth, beauty, justice, knowledge, life, art, education, happiness, love

These abstract nouns are noncount nouns, but the fact that a noun is abstract does not necessarily mean that it is also a noncount noun. The following is a little thought experiment that shows how difficult it is to intuitively distinguish count from noncount abstract nouns. All of the following ten words are abstract nouns. Five are count nouns and five are noncount nouns. How many can you correctly identify?

NOUN	COUNT OR NONCOUNT?
sorrow	_____
assistance	_____
failure	_____
luck	_____
outcome	_____
advice	_____
decision	_____
truth	_____
progress	_____
risk	_____

Answers, in alphabetical order: *advice*, noncount; *assistance*, noncount; *decision*, count; *failure*, count; *luck*, noncount; *outcome*, count; *progress*, noncount; *risk*, count; *sorrow*, count; *truth*, noncount.

The following are some helpful categories of abstract noncount nouns. As we would expect, nearly all the categories are based on the meaning of the nouns, but the most common category is based on grammar.

Abstract noncount nouns derived from adjectives by the suffix -*ness*

Most adjectives can be changed into abstract nouns by adding the suffix -*ness*. This is the largest definable group of abstract noncount nouns (more than 800 in total, though many are low frequency). The following are some examples:

ADJECTIVE	NOUN
attractive	attractiveness
cool	coolness
false	falseness
lazy	laziness
ripe	ripeness
smooth	smoothness

Virtually all of these derived nouns are noncount.

> We couldn't help but notice the **X** coolnesses of the delegation members.
> The **X** quicknesses of their passes made them a hard team to beat.
> The **X** willingnesses of the children to help made a real difference.

Activities

This large group of nouns representing activities has three subcategories:

-ing activity words

These -*ing* words are all gerunds, which are present participles used as abstract nouns: *working, hiking, playing, reading, singing, sleeping.* The following are some examples in sentences:

> <u>Working</u> from home is a real blessing for new parents.
> Their <u>playing</u> has improved greatly over the last few months.

When we try to use the -*ing* word in the plural, the result is ungrammatical:

> **X** <u>Workings</u> from home are a real blessing for new parents.
> Their **X** <u>playings</u> have improved greatly over the last few months.

Academic disciplines and professions

Examples of the abstract noncount nouns for academic disciplines and professions include *art, biology, chemistry, economics, engineering, history, research, linguistics, literature, mathematics, music, physics, poetry, psychology, science,* and *medicine.*

> These terms are ungrammatical if used in the plural:

> We are studying the **X** <u>histories</u> of the first Americans.
> Their **X** <u>literatures</u> have generated a lot of interest.

Sports and games

The names for nearly all sports and games are abstract noncount nouns: *chess, checkers, bridge, poker, football, baseball, soccer,* and *tennis.*

> These terms are ungrammatical if used in the plural:

> Many retired people play **X** <u>bridges</u> several times a week.
> **X** <u>Baseballs</u> are played everywhere in Japan.

Natural phenomena

Most forces and events in the natural world are noncount nouns. Here are some examples: *electricity, gravity, weather, heat, cold, humidity, rain, thunder, lightning, cold, frost, time,* and *weight.*

> These terms are ungrammatical if used in the plural:

> The **X** <u>heats</u> and **X** <u>humidities</u> in the summer are almost unbearable.
> The **X** <u>gravities</u> on other planets can be quite different from Earth's.

To summarize, we have discussed three categories of abstract noncount nouns in this section:

1. Abstract noncount nouns derived from adjectives by the suffix *-ness*

2. Activities

  ◆ *-ing* activity words
  ◆ Academic disciplines and professions
  ◆ Sports and games

3. Natural phenomena

Identifying the three main categories of abstract noncount nouns *All of the underlined words in the following sentences are abstract noncount nouns. Decide whether the noun is (a) a derived noun ending in –ness, (b) an activity word, or (c) a natural phenomena word. Three examples are given.*

Every physical object has <u>mass</u>.

(c) natural phenomena

<u>Cleanliness</u> is next to godliness. (saying)

(a) derived noun ending in -ness

<u>Seeing</u> is <u>believing</u>. (saying)

(b) activity word

1. Access to <u>music</u> and <u>art</u> is a real benefit of living in the city.

2. We hardly ever get <u>rain</u> during the summer.

3. <u>Taking</u> vacations actually improves worker productivity.

4. Battery technology is a balance between <u>power</u> and <u>weight</u>.

5. I read mostly <u>fiction</u>.

_____

6. Too much TV can cause <u>sleeplessness</u>.

_____

7. <u>Astronomy</u> has almost become a branch of <u>physics</u>.

_____

8. <u>Lightning</u> and <u>thunder</u> scare my dog to death.

_____

9. <u>Driving</u> so many hours at a time gives me terrific backaches.

_____

10. Increasing the <u>awareness</u> of the dangers of smoking has been very important.

_____

The definite
article *the*

The definite article *the* is not only the most common article, but also the most commonly used word in English—twice as common, in fact, as the next most common word, the verb *be*. We will first examine the pronunciation of *the* and then its meaning and uses.

The pronunciation of *the*

Like all articles, *the* is normally unstressed. It is pronounced /ðə/ (rhymes with *duh*) before words beginning with a consonant sound:

> the /ðə/ team
> the /ðə/ bridge
> the /ðə/ song

The is pronounced /ðiy/ (rhymes with *see*) before words beginning with a vowel sound:

> the /ðiy/ accident
> the /ðiy/ example
> the /ðiy/ orange

Note: If *the* before a consonant sound is given extra emphasis, it is pronounced /ðiy/ instead of the expected /ðə/, as in the following sentence:

> She was probably **the** /ðiy/ best player I ever coached.

In all of our discussion about the pronunciation of *the*, we assume (unless stated otherwise) that we are talking about the normal, unstressed pronunciation of *the*.

Pronunciation of *the* *Indicate the correct pronunciation of unstressed* the *with the following nouns. An example is provided.*

NOUN	/ðə/	/ðiy/
question	X	_____
1. umbrella	_____	_____
2. desk	_____	_____
3. name	_____	_____
4. insurance	_____	_____
5. eraser	_____	_____
6. test	_____	_____
7. road	_____	_____
8. action	_____	_____
9. building	_____	_____
10. organization	_____	_____

The main problem nonnative speakers have with the pronunciation of *the* is when the word after *the* has a spelling that can mislead. The most common mispronunciations of *the* are with words that begin with the letter *u* or *h*.

Typically, words beginning with the letter *u* are pronounced with a vowel sound, most often with the schwa sound, /ə/, as in *under* or the negative prefix *un-*. As we would expect, unstressed *the* is usually pronounced /ðə/ with these words, for example: /ðə/ *underpass*, /ðə/ *ugliness*, /ðə/ *upper floors*, /ðə/ *Urdu language*, /ðə/ *utterance*.

Note: Native speakers pronounce *the* inconsistently, so you will occasionally hear /ðiy/ pronunciations where you would expect /ðə/.

About fifty words beginning with the letter *u* actually begin with the consonant *y* sound as in the initial sound of the words *yeast* and *yesterday*. Because these words begin with a consonant sound, the article *the* is pronounced /ðə/ with these words rather than the expected /ðiy/. Many of these exceptional words are related to the word *unit*, for example: *union, unity, universe,* and *uniform* are all pronounced with the consonant *y*, so that *the* is pronounced /ðə/: /ðə/ *unit*, /ðə/ *union*, /ðə/ *unity*, /ðə/ *universe*, and /ðə/ *uniform*. A few words unrelated to *unit* are pronounced with an initial *y* sound: /ðə/

ukulele, /ðə/ *utopia*, and /ðə/ *use* (the noun, rhyming with *noose*, not the verb *use*, rhyming with *ooze*.)

Over time, a few words spelled with the initial letter *h* have lost their initial consonant *h* sound so that these words now begin with a vowel sound. For example, the words *honor*, *honesty*, and *herb* now begin with vowel sounds. Consequently we pronounce *the* with these words as /ðiy/: /ðiy/ *honor*, /ðiy/ *honesty*, and /ðiy/ *herb*. Many words related to the word *heir* are no longer pronounced with an initial *h* sound: /ðiy/ *heir*, /ðiy/ *heiress*, and /ðiy/ *heirloom*.

There is a tendency for four-syllable words beginning with *h* to drop the initial consonant so that these words are used with /ðiy/:

/ðiy/ Hysterical passengers fled the scene of the accident.

EXERCISE

2·2

Pronunciation of *the* before words beginning with *u* and *h* Indicate the correct pronunciation of unstressed *the* with the following nouns. Two examples are provided.

NOUN	/ðə/	/ðiy/
university	_____	X
house	X	_____
1. unicorn	_____	_____
2. honor	_____	_____
3. happiness	_____	_____
4. ultimate	_____	_____
5. horror	_____	_____
6. humble	_____	_____
7. utensils	_____	_____
8. upset	_____	_____
9. hunger	_____	_____
10. honest	_____	_____

One place where nonnative speakers often use the wrong pronunciation for *the* is when pronouncing the names of individual letters or when pronouncing certain types of acronyms that spell out abbreviations letter-by-letter like *UN* (United Nations), *BBC* (British Broadcasting Corporation), *GRE* (Graduate Record Examinations), and *ESL* (English as a second language)—as opposed to acronyms like *AIDS* (acquired immunodeficiency syndrome), *NATO* (North Atlantic Treaty Organization), and *UNICEF* (United Nations Children's Fund) that break the acronym into pronounceable syllables.

As you would expect, if the name of the letter begins with a consonant sound, we pronounce *the* as /ðə/, and if the name of the letter begins with a vowel sound, we pronounce *the* as /ðiy/. So far, so good. The problem is that there is no necessary connection between the names of the letters and their pronunciations. To take the most extreme example, the name for the letter *w* is double-*u*, which describes the shape of the letter and has nothing to do with the sound of the letter. A more common problem is that the names of some consonants actually begin with vowel sounds rather than with consonant sounds as one would expect. (The consonant *f* is pronounced with a vowel that rhymes with *deaf*.) Since the pronunciation of the letter's name begins with a vowel sound, not a consonant sound, we say /ðiy/ *f* rather than the /ðə/ *f*.

The following table shows whether the names of the twenty-six letters begin with a consonant or vowel sound and gives the correct pronunciation of *the* and the letter.

LETTER	BEGINS WITH	PRONUNCIATION OF *THE*
A	vowel	/ðiy/ *a* rhymes with *say*
B	consonant	/ðə/ *b*
C	consonant	/ðə/ *c*
D	consonant	/ðə/ *d*
E	vowel	/ðiy/ *e* rhymes with *see*
F	vowel	/ðiy/ *f*
G	consonant	/ðə/ *g*
H	vowel	/ðiy/ *h* /eyc‡/
I	vowel	/ðiy/ *i* rhymes with *my*
J	consonant	/ðə/ *j*
K	consonant	/ðə/ *k*
L	vowel	/ðiy/ *l* rhymes with *sell*
M	vowel	/ðiy/ *m* rhymes with *him*
N	vowel	/ðiy/ *n* rhymes with *hen*
O	vowel	/ðiy/ *o* rhymes with *go*
P	consonant	/ðə/ *p*
Q	consonant	/ðə/ *q* (pronounced /kyuw/ as in the word *cute*.)
R	vowel	/ðiy/ *r* rhymes with *far*
S	vowel	/ðiy/ *s* rhymes with *yes*
T	consonant	/ðə/*t*
U	consonant	/ðə/ *u* rhymes with *few*
V	consonant	/ðə/ *v*

(continued)

LETTER	BEGINS WITH	PRONUNCIATION OF *THE*
W	consonant	/ðə/ *w* pronounced "double /yuw/"
X	vowel	/ðiy/ *x*
Y	consonant	/ðə/ *y* rhymes with *my*
Z	consonant	/ðə/ *z*

EXERCISE

2·3

Pronunciation of *the* before acronyms that use the names of letters *Select the proper phonetic symbol for the correct pronunciation of* the *preceding the acronyms in each of the following sentences. Two examples are provided:*

She works for the /ðə/ /ðiy/ HHS. (Department of Health and Human Services)

She works for the /ðiy/ HHS. (Department of Health and Human Services)

The /ðə/ /ðiy/ FHA (Federal Housing Administration) insures bank loans for home building.

The /ðə/ FHA (Federal Housing Administration) insures bank loans for home building.

1. The /ðə/ /ðiy/ CEO (chief executive officer) of their company just resigned.

2. I am enrolling in the /ðə/ /ðiy/ MBA (master of business administration) program.

3. The /ðə/ /ðiy/ hospital is run by the VA (Department of Veterans Affairs).

4. They live in the /ðə/ /ðiy/ UK (United Kingdom).

5. I go to an exercise class at the /ðə/ /ðiy/ YMCA (Young Men's Christian Association).

6. We watched the /ðə/ /ðiy/ LPGA (Ladies Professional Golf Association) tournament Saturday.

7. The /ðə/ /ðiy/ ROI (return on investment) has more than met expectations.

8. The vaccination program was sponsored by the /ðə/ /ðiy/ WHO (World Health Organization).

9. The /ðə/ /ðiy/ CAD (computer-aided design) program is going to cost a fortune.

10. The /ðə/ /ðiy/ EPA (Environmental Protection Agency) must approve the plan.

The meaning and use of *the*

The is the least restricted article in its use. It is the only article that can be freely used with all three categories of nouns: singular count nouns, plural count nouns, and noncount nouns.

SINGULAR COUNT NOUN:	*The* bridge is icy.
PLURAL COUNT NOUN:	*The* bridges are icy.
NONCOUNT NOUN:	*The* existence of black holes is well established.

It is also unique in that it is the only article that can be extensively used with proper nouns—the names of individual people and places.

Typically, we do not use the definite article with the names of individual people unless there is a post-noun modifier that provides some special information about that person. Compare the following sentences:

> *John* went on vacation last week.
> **The** *John* who works in accounting went on vacation last week.

The use of the post-noun modifier *who works in accounting* indentifies the specific person named John that the speaker is talking about. In this case, the use of the definite article becomes obligatory.

One of the few instances in which we regularly use the definite article with names is for titles, both royal titles and organizational titles:

ROYAL AND POLITICAL TITLES:	the Duke of York, the Prince of Wales, the Prime Minister
ORGANIZATION TITLES:	the president, the treasurer, the CEO, the secretary

By far the most common use of *the* with proper nouns is for place names. Plural place names are typically used with *the*. Two especially common categories are the names of mountain ranges and island chains:

MOUNTAIN RANGES:	the Alps, the Andes, the Himalayas, the Rockies
ISLAND CHAINS:	the Aleutians, the Azores, the Philippines, the Shetlands

The use of *the* with singular place names is much more inconsistent. Here are some categories of singular place names that are typically used with the definite article:

BODIES OF WATER (RIVERS, SEAS, OCEANS, CANALS):	the Columbia, the Mississippi, the Potomac, the Thames, the Atlantic, the Bay of Bengal, the Gulf of California, the Erie Canal, the Hood Canal, the Panama Canal

PUBLIC FACILITIES, MONUMENTS, BUILDINGS, HOTELS, THEATERS, BRIDGES, ESPECIALLY IF WELL KNOWN:	the Marriott, the Ritz, the Waldorf Astoria, the Apollo, the Globe, the Met, the Roxie, the Brooklyn Bridge, the Chesapeake Bay Bridge, the Golden Gate Bridge, the Lincoln Memorial, the Tomb of the Unknown Soldier, the British Museum, the Getty, the Library of Congress

EXERCISE 2·4

Using *the* with proper nouns *All of the proper nouns in the following sentences have been underlined. Add* the *to proper nouns that require definite articles. Add ∅, the zero article, to proper nouns that do not require definite articles. Two examples are provided.*

Mount St. Helens in Washington State erupted violently in 1980.

∅ Mount St. Helens in ∅ Washington State erupted violently in 1980.

Receptionist suggested that I contact director of admissions.

The receptionist suggested that I contact **the** director of admissions.

1. Air Force Academy is located in Colorado Springs.

2. A snow storm in Cascades has closed Highway I-90.

3. Washington Monument is the tallest structure in Washington, DC.

4. Dr. Brown whom I was talking about is our dentist.

5. The company is replacing treasurer in July.

6. Faroe Islands are off the coast of Norway.

7. Easter is unusually early this year.

8. Sacramento is the longest river in California.

_____

9. The English novelist G. K. Chesterton wrote many mystery stories featuring Father Brown.

_____

10. Christmas I was talking about must have been when we were still living on Ellsworth Street.

_____

The usual meaning and use of the definite article *the* with ordinary common nouns is governed by two rules. Use the definite article *the* if and only if *both* of the following statements about the noun being modified are true: (1) you (the speaker or writer) have a specific person, place, thing, or idea in mind, *and* (2) you (the speaker or writer) can reasonably assume that the intended listener or reader will know which specific person, place, thing, or idea you mean. The second statement is the critical requirement: that the listener or reader can be reasonably assumed to know *which* noun you are referring to.

In practice, the second requirement is usually met in one of the following four ways:

◆ previous mention
◆ defined by modifiers
◆ normal expectations
◆ uniqueness

Previous mention

Use the definite article *the* with a particular noun if you have already introduced the noun to the listener or reader in a previous sentence:

> I just got a new camera. *The* camera has an image stabilization feature.

The definite article *the* is used in the second sentence because the noun *camera* was introduced in the first sentence, and thus we can reasonably assume that the listener or reader will know which camera we are talking about in the second sentence.

> PERSON A: Do we have any stamps?
> PERSON B: The stamps are kept at the receptionist's desk.

In this example, Person B uses the definite article because the noun *stamps* has been introduced by Person A's question. The first mention of a noun establishes its identity.

All subsequent references to that same noun use *the* to signal that this is still the same noun that was established earlier.

Defined by modifiers

Even if a noun has not been previously mentioned, use the definite article if the noun is followed by modifiers that serve to uniquely identify it. Here are two examples where the noun is modified by adjective (relative) clauses:

> Did you see *the* movie that is showing at the Roxie?

The noun *movie* is uniquely defined by the modifier *that is showing at the Roxie.*

> *The* assignment I just got in calculus is a real killer.

The noun *assignment* is uniquely defined by the modifier *I just got in calculus.*
   The modifier does not need to be a full adjective clause. It can be as simple as a prepositional phrase:

> *The* store in the village is closed on Sundays.

In this example the noun *store* is uniquely defined by the prepositional phrase *in the village.*

Normal expectations

Use the definite article if the noun is something the reader can reasonably expect from the context of the sentence even if there has been no previous mention of the noun. This important use of the definite article is often not understood by nonnative speakers:

> I opened a book and checked *the* index. (We expect books to have indexes.)
> *The* screen on my new computer is flickering. (We expect computers to have screens.)
> A storm far out to sea was making *the* waves higher than normal. (We expect the sea to have waves.)
> I love my new car, but *the* brakes are pretty squeaky. (We expect cars to have brakes.)

There is a large and quite idiomatic extension of this usage with names of places, which we will discuss later.

Uniqueness

We use *the* with things that we already know about because they are unique. Some things are unique because they are physically or logically unique, for example, *the sun, the moon, the horizon, the earth, the north pole, the future,* and *the past.* More frequently, however, we come across things that are unique in a particular context or situation. For example, if there is only one freeway in town, we would always use *the* because it is unique, even though there has been no previous mention of the freeway in the conversation. For example,

> They live on the other side of the freeway.

If you were in the shower and you heard the telephone ringing, you might call out, "Can somebody answer *the* phone?" The word *phone* has not been previously mentioned, but in this context the ringing of the phone makes it unique.

If there were a major sporting event taking place, everyone would know what a speaker meant when he or she said, "Who's winning *the* game?" The noun *game* is defined by its uniqueness in that context.

EXERCISE

2·5

Four reasons for using the definite article *the* *All of the underlined uses of* the *in the following sentences are grammatical. For each sentence, identify the reason for using the definite article: (a) previous mention, (b) defined by modifiers, (c) normal expectations, or (d) uniqueness. Four examples are provided.*

A car cut right in front us, and then the car ran through a red light.

(a) previous mention

No one recognized the handwriting used on the outside of the envelope.

(b) defined by modifiers

The bathroom sink was plugged up again.

(c) normal expectations (We expect bathrooms to have sinks.)

Tides at the equator are very small.

(d) uniqueness

1. We finally repaid the loan we got from my parents when we were first married.

____

2. The house was OK, but the kitchen was small and dark.

____

3. There was a policeman at the door. Ms. White asked <u>the</u> policeman what he wanted.

_____

4. <u>The</u> heroines in books always seem to be young and beautiful.

_____

5. Everyone is concerned about increasing pollution in <u>the</u> atmosphere.

_____

6. We went into an office building and took <u>the</u> elevator to <u>the</u> top floor.

_____

7. <u>The</u> pier at Sunset Beach has a Ferris wheel and a roller coaster.

_____

8. There were some tools left on the porch. I asked everyone if they knew whom <u>the</u> tools belonged to.

_____

9. I opened some books and quickly went through <u>the</u> table of contents.

_____

10. I had trouble with <u>the</u> questions about compound interest rates.

_____

English extends the concept of **normal expectations** to a surprising extent with common nouns that refer to places. Here is a typical example: Suppose you are out having lunch with a friend, and the two of you are starting to go back to your office. Your friend stops and says, "Oh, I forgot. Excuse me for a minute. I have to go to *the bank*." There has been no previous mention of the word *bank*. There is no bank in sight. Why then did your friend use the definite article *the* with *bank*? The use of *the* seems to violate the cardinal rule for using the definite article that you (the speaker or writer) can reasonably assume the intended listener or reader will know which specific person, place, thing, or idea you mean. But in this case the listener has no idea which bank the speaker is talking about. So why is this usage not only grammatical but customary?

The reason is a remarkable broadening of *normal expectations* to include places that you would expect to find in a particular environment. You expect to find banks in a city or any urban environment. The following examples are grouped by environment:

At a university

I have to go to   *the* bookstore.
the dean's office.
the cafeteria.
the library.
the registrar's office.

In a city

I have to go to   *the* post office.
the bank.
the train station.
the airport.
the drugstore.

If you were in a city in England, you could also say, "Let's go to *the* pub."

On a ranch or farm

I have to go to   *the* barn.
the feedlot.
the stables.
the chicken coop.
the vegetable garden.

There is a similar odd use of *the* with the names of places of recreation:

Let's go to   *the* beach.
the movies.
the mountains.
the park.

Even though the listener has no way of knowing which movie or park the speaker has in mind (if, in fact, the speaker has any particular one in mind), it is still conventional to use the definite article with these nouns.

The singular indefinite article *a/an*

The literal meaning of the word *indefinite* is "not definite." In grammar, an indefinite article is used to signal that the noun it modifies has *not* been defined or determined. The definite article *the* is the opposite. It is used to signal that the noun it modifies has already been defined or determined. Compare the underlined articles in the following sentences:

DEFINITE ARTICLE:	Do you have the pencil?
INDEFINITE ARTICLE:	Do you have a pencil?

In the first sentence, the use of the definite article *the* tells the audience that the noun it modifies has already been defined or determined. In the second sentence, the use of the indefinite article *a* tells the audience that the noun it modifies has not been defined or determined.

A versus *an*

Singular count nouns are used with the indefinite articles *a* and *an*. The reason why the singular count noun has two forms is historical. Both *a* and *an* come from the word *one*. Over the years, the unstressed pronunciation of *one* used as a noun modifier (as opposed to the use of *one* used as number word) became contracted: the *n* in *one* was preserved before words beginning with vowel sounds and lost before words beginning with consonant sounds. So the unstressed modifier *one* in the phrase *one rock* contracted to *a rock* and in the phrase *one apple* contracted to *an apple*.

The rule governing the use of *an* pertains to vowel pronunciation, not vowel spelling. The following words use *a* where the spelling would seem to require *an* because the pronunciation of the nouns actually begins with a /y/-consonant sound, not a vowel sound:

a unicorn
a uniform
a unit

34

> *a* university
>
> *a* usage

Most of the words beginning with the letter *u* are formed with prefixes, especially the prefixes *un-* and *under-* as in *unfair* and *undercoat*. Words beginning with the prefixes *un-* and *under-* never begin with a /y/-consonant sound, so we know that these words will always be used with *an*:

> *an* unapproved expense
>
> *an* unarmed policeman
>
> *an* unconfirmed statement
>
> *an* underdog
>
> *an* undergraduate
>
> *an* underground cable
>
> *an* undershirt
>
> *an* unfair advantage

The reverse can also happen. Sometimes we use *an* where the spelling would seem to require *a* because the initial consonant *h* is not pronounced, causing the word to actually begin with a vowel sound. Here are the most common nouns and adjectives where the *h* is lost:

> *an* heir
>
> *an* heiress
>
> *an* heirloom
>
> *an* honest mistake
>
> *an* honor
>
> *an* honorarium
>
> *an* honorary degree
>
> *an* honorable thing to do
>
> *an* hour
>
> *an* hourly rate

EXERCISE
3·1

A and *an* with singular count nouns *Use the appropriate form of the articles a/an with the singular count nouns in the following sentences. Two examples are given.*

It has been _____ honor to work with you.

It has been *an* honor to work with you.

Her first job was at _____ university in Australia.

Her first job was at *a* university in Australia.

1. Her mother was _____ heir to _____ huge ranch in west Texas.

2. They had _____ advantage that we were never able to overcome.

3. We expect _____ announcement to be made within _____ hour or two.

4. It was _____ ideal solution as far as I was concerned.

5. _____ apple _____ day keeps the doctor away. (saying)

6. It is _____ usage that we just don't hear much anymore.

7. _____ attorney for the opposition raised _____ objection we had not expected.

8. That is _____ altogether different thing.

9. It was _____ honest difference of opinion.

10. She held _____ honorary position at _____ university in her native country.

The meaning and use of the singular indefinite article *a/an*

As the name *singular indefinite article* tells us, we must use *a/an* with singular nouns. What is not so obvious is why we cannot use the *a/an* with noncount nouns. After all, noncount nouns can never be used in the plural, so all noncount nouns must be singular. So why can't we use the singular article *a/an* with noncount nouns?

The simple answer is that *a/an* is a contracted form of the number word *one*, and we know that we cannot use number words with noncount nouns. In the following examples, the number word *one* and the indefinite article *a/an* are equally ungrammatical with noncount nouns:

> There is **X** one dirt all over the garage floor.
> There is **X** a dirt all over the garage floor.
> I have **X** one advice for you.
> I have **X** an advice for you.

A more sophisticated answer is that when we attach a number to a noun, we are enumerating specific instances of that noun. In the sentence,

> I got <u>four</u> apples at the store on my way home.

we are enumerating four apples. Likewise, we can enumerate the occurrence of a single apple:

> I got one apple at the store on my way home.

And we can use the indefinite article *a/an* to enumerate the occurrence of a single apple:

> I got an apple at the store on my way home.

However, noncount nouns can never be individually enumerated, because noncount nouns are entire, undividable categories of things or ideas that can never be enumerated as specific instances of a count noun.

What can be confusing about noncount nouns is that despite how noncount nouns can never be enumerated as single nouns, they function as singular nouns in terms of subject-verb agreement. For example, in the sentence,

> Our company's software is very advanced.

the subject of the sentence, *software*, is a noncount noun, yet it enters into a subject-verb agreement relationship with the singular verb *is*. Doesn't that mean that the noncount noun *software* is a singular noun? Well, yes and no. There is a fundamental grammatical requirement that for a sentence to be a sentence, the subject and the appropriate verb must enter into a valid subject-verb relationship. So in this technical grammatical sense, the noncount noun *software* functions as a singular noun, but solely for the purpose of subject-verb agreement. However, semantically, the noun *software*, like all noncount nouns, has no number at all. It is neither singular nor plural—it is numberless.

A common use of the indefinite article *a/an* is to signal to the audience that the speaker or writer is introducing a specific new topic or subject matter to the discourse. This topic, after it has been introduced with the indefinite article *a/an*, will then be used with the definite article *the* in all subsequent conversation or writing:

> I just got a new book on Lincoln. The book is one of the best histories of the period I have ever read. The book deals mainly with Lincoln's relationship with the men he ran against for the presidency.

The key difference between the indefinite article and the definite article is that the use of the indefinite article tells the audience that the noun it modifies is new information, while the use of the definite article tells the audience that the noun it modifies is already known to them.

Probably, for Americans at least, the most famous specific use of the indefinite article was during the flight of *Apollo 13*, a manned flight to the moon. Before the flight reached the moon, an oxygen tank aboard the rocket exploded. The crew notified the flight base in Houston about the accident with the now-famous phrase, "Houston, we have a problem." (Actually, the famous phrase is a slight misquotation. What they really said was, "Houston, we have had a problem.") The indefinite article is used to signal the introduction of a specific topic that will be new to the audience but, of course, is already known to the speaker or writer.

The following are some more prosaic examples of using the indefinite article to introduce a specific new topic:

> Can I ask you a question?
> We went to a great restaurant last night.
> Did you see an orange notebook in the conference room?
> He gave us a good piece of advice.

We often use the existential *there* (meaning "there exists") with the indefinite article to introduce a specific new subject:

> There is a mosquito in the bedroom.
> There is a problem I have been meaning to talk to you about.
> There is a strange car parked in the driveway.

We can even use the indefinite article for proper nouns. For example, it would be appropriate in the following situation. A previously unknown person by the name of Mr. Jones comes to your office and asks the receptionist to speak to you. The receptionist would call you and probably say, "There is a Mr. Jones here to see you." If the receptionist had just said, "Mr. Jones is here to see you," it would imply that the receptionist expects you to already know who Mr. Jones is. Since the receptionist knows that you do not know who Mr. Jones is, the receptionist uses the indefinite article to signal that the person is known to the speaker, but is *not* known to the audience, extending the use of the indefinite article to a proper noun. The following are some more examples of proper nouns used with indefinite articles:

> There is a New York that tourists never see.
> Some economists expect to see a Europe that is in steep economic decline.
> My grandmother remembers a Princeton that no longer exists.

The indefinite article has several other uses besides the main use of introducing a specific new topic. By far the most important of these is using the indefinite article to introduce a new **nonspecific** topic. In the sentence,

> Do you know a good dentist?

the speaker is introducing a new topic, but does not have a single, specific individual or thing in mind. Rather, the new topic is a category of people or things, not a specific person or thing:

> The Marines are looking for a few good men. (advertising slogan)
> You look like you need a friend.
> We would love to find an apartment in New York that we could actually afford.

The fact that there are two uses of the indefinite article often creates ambiguity in conversation. For example, if a friend said, "Let's go out to a movie tonight," the audience does not know if (1) the speaker is thinking of a specific movie that the speaker wants to see (specific indefinite article) or if (2) the speaker does not have a specific movie in mind (nonspecific indefinite article) and is making a broader suggestion of going to the movies (as a category of activity). The natural response of the audience to the question would be to clarify the speaker's intended meaning by asking, "Did you have a particular movie in mind you want to see?" Many questions that use the indefinite article run the risk of this kind of ambiguity: the audience cannot tell whether the speaker's use of an indefinite article is intended as a specific or a nonspecific article.

The following bit of dialogue is prompted by the distinction between the two kinds of indefinite articles:

CUSTOMER: I'll just have a salad.
WAITER: What kind would you like?
CUSTOMER: I don't know. What do you have?

The waiter's question is prompted by the ambiguity of the indefinite article in the customer's request. The waiter does not know if the customer has something specific in mind or not. The customer's response tells us that the indefinite article was definitely nonspecific—the customer did not have any specific type of salad in mind.

There are two special uses of the nonspecific indefinite article. The first is to characterize or define someone or something as a member of a class. In the sentence,

> A kohlrabi is a variety of cabbage.

the indefinite article does not refer to a single, specific kohlrabi, but rather is used to define kohlrabi as a member of the cabbage family. The following are some more examples of this "characterizing" use of the nonspecific indefinite article:

> An ophthalmologist is a doctor who specializes in the treatment of eye disorders and diseases.
> A Miata is a sports car made by Mazda.
> His wife is a doctor at our clinic.

The second use of the nonspecific indefinite article is to talk in general terms or to make generalizations. In the sentence,

> To ensure a good camping trip, always prepare for the worst possible weather.

the speaker is not thinking about any one actual camping trip. The speaker is using the nonspecific indefinite article to signal that the speaker is making a generalization about all camping trips. The following are more examples:

> A ripe melon will sound a little hollow when thumped.
> A close game is always exciting to watch.

One of the greatest health risks for the elderly is a fall.
In case of an emergency, do not use the elevators.

Traditional sayings and aphorisms often use the nonspecific indefinite article to make generalizations about categories of things or people. Here is an exercise just for fun, with ten traditional sayings that nearly all native speaker adults know. (Children, especially younger children, are often completely mystified by these expressions.) How many of these expressions have you heard?

1. An ounce of prevention is worth a pound of cure.

2. A fool and his money are soon parted.

3. A stitch in time saves nine.

4. It is an ill wind that blows no good.

5. A friend in need is a friend indeed.

6. An apple a day keeps the doctor away.

7. A watched pot never boils.

8. A bird in the hand is worth two in the bush.

9. A man's house is his castle.

10. A picture is worth a thousand words.

Some of these sayings are so well-known that people often just use the first half, knowing that the audience will fill in the rest of the saying:

An ounce of prevention . . .
A fool and his money . . .
A friend in need . . .
A bird in the hand . . .

Often when we use nonspecific indefinite articles to make generalizations, the noun we are talking about is actually a metaphor for something else. Here is a saying from the New Testament famously used by Abraham Lincoln in reference to the conflicts between the North and the South just prior to the Civil War:

A house divided against itself cannot stand.

Lincoln was not talking about a specific house. In fact, he was not talking about a house at all. Rather he was using the noun *house* as a metaphor representing the entire nation.

A summary of indefinite article uses

A basic function of the indefinite article is to signal the audience that the speaker or writer is introducing a new topic to the discourse. We use the indefinite article in two different ways. Most of the time we use the indefinite article to introduce a specific new topic that will be further elaborated. We have called an article of this type a **specific indefinite article**. Sometimes, however, we use the indefinite article in a broader way to express a general feeling or make a general comment without any specific person or thing in mind. We have called an article of this type a **nonspecific indefinite article**.

SPECIFIC INDEFINITE ARTICLE:	We should get a birthday card for Dan.
NONSPECIFIC INDEFINITE ARTICLE:	I need a breath of air. (Obviously the speaker does not have one specific breath of air in mind. In fact, the speaker may not be talking about air at all, but about the need to take a break.)

Often in conversation, the type of indefinite article intended by the speaker is ambiguous because the audience cannot tell from the statement which of the two types of indefinite article the speaker intended. That is, the audience does not know whether the speaker has a specific person or thing in mind or not:

We need to stop at a filling station.

The speaker could have one specific filling station in mind (specific indefinite article) or not (nonspecific definite article), in which case the speaker could be content to stop at any filling station, probably the first one he or she comes to.

The nonspecific indefinite article has two additional uses:

1. To characterize or define someone or something as a member of a class. Many definitions use nonspecific indefinite articles:

   A sentence expresses a complete thought and must contain a subject and a verb.

2. To make generalizations. We use the nonspecific indefinite article to talk in general terms or to make generalizations:

   A good test not only assesses the students' abilities, but also teaches them something about the content.

The sentence is not talking about any actual test, but is making a generalization about the nature of good tests.

The four uses of indefinite articles *Each of the following sentences contains an underlined indefinite article. Pick which of the four uses of the indefinite article best describes the underlined indefinite articles: (a) introduce specific new topic, (b) introduce nonspecific new topic, (c) characterize or define, or (d) make generalizations. Four examples are given.*

I think I have a broken bone in my left hand.

(a) introduce specific new topic

Everyone needs to have a dream.

(b) introduce nonspecific new topic

My dog is a golden retriever.

(c) characterize or define

A small town is a great place to bring up a family.

(d) make generalizations

1. If you are starting a business, you must make a revenue plan.

   _____

2. The company is a subsidiary of ADM.

   _____

3. The children were frightened by a strange noise coming from the attic.

   _____

4. A contract is a legal obligation.

   _____

5. I met a friend of yours yesterday.

   _____

6. There is never a policeman around when you need one.

   _____

7. The book is about a disputed election.

   _____

8. <u>A</u> good man is hard to find. (saying)

_____

9. The person renting the cottage is <u>a</u> retired schoolteacher.

_____

10. Everybody needs <u>a</u> helping hand once in a while.

_____

The indefinite article *some*

Some is used with two different categories of nouns: plural count nouns and noncount nouns. Here are examples of both uses:

Plural nouns
We had to get **some** new <u>maps</u> for the trip.
We need **some** extra <u>keys</u> made for the new house.

Noncount nouns
We heard **some** <u>thunder</u> last night, but we didn't get any rain.
There is **some** <u>fruit</u> in the refrigerator.

When the indefinite plural article *some* is used with plural count nouns, *some* is the semantic counterpart of the singular indefinite article *a/an*, for example:

SINGULAR INDEFINITE ARTICLE:	We got <u>a</u> new client yesterday.
PLURAL INDEFINITE ARTICLE:	We got <u>some</u> new clients yesterday.

For this reason, *some* is sometimes treated as the plural equivalent of the singular article *a/an*, so that family of articles looks like this:

DEFINITE ARTICLE:	the
INDEFINITE ARTICLES:	a/an (*s.*) some (*pl.*)

However, in terms of meaning and use, there is no difference between *some* used with plural count nouns and *some* used with noncount nouns. Everything discussed about *some* in this section holds equally for plural count nouns and noncount nouns. In the same way that *the* is used identically with all three categories of nouns, *some* is used identically with plural count nouns and noncount nouns.

Some is unique among the articles because *some*, unlike the articles *the* and *a/an*, can be turned into an indefinite pronoun by deleting the noun that *some* modifies. Obviously the conversion of the indefinite article *some* to the indefinite pronoun *some* depends on the reference of the indefinite pronoun being clear to the audience from context. Here are several examples with the indefinite article *some* changed into the indefinite pronoun *some*:

Plural count nouns

INDEFINITE ARTICLE:	<u>Some</u> students take the bus.
INDEFINITE PRONOUN:	<u>Some</u> ~~students~~ take the bus.
INDEFINITE ARTICLE:	We need to return <u>some</u> plants.
INDEFINITE PRONOUN:	We need to return <u>some</u> ~~plants~~.

Noncount nouns

INDEFINITE ARTICLE:	We hope to get <u>some</u> rain tomorrow.
INDEFINITE PRONOUN:	We hope to get <u>some</u> ~~rain~~ tomorrow.
INDEFINITE ARTICLE:	<u>Some</u> information is always lost in transmission.
INDEFINITE PRONOUN:	<u>Some</u> ~~information~~ is always lost in transmission.

We often change the indefinite article *some* into the indefinite pronoun *some* to avoid repeating the noun modified by the indefinite article. In the following sentence,

I'm making a fresh pot of coffee. Would you like <u>some</u>?

the speaker does not want to repeat the noun *coffee*, which if the speaker did, would make the following perfectly grammatical but very odd-sounding sentence:

I'm making a fresh pot of coffee. Would you like <u>some</u> coffee?

The repetition of the noun *coffee* makes it sound like the speaker is talking to two different people rather than the same person.

Idiomatic uses of the indefinite article *some*

Before discussing the main uses and meaning of the indefinite article *some*, we need to identify and then set aside three idiomatic uses of the indefinite article *some*. Fortunately, these uses are so distinctive in form or meaning that they are easily recognized.

Approximation

In this use, *some* functions as an adverb of approximation when we estimate amount—weight, money, time, percentages, and so on. It means "nearly," "about," or "roughly." For example:

The trail gains <u>some</u> 400 feet in elevation over its length.
The challenger is winning by <u>some</u> 500 votes at the moment.
Only <u>some</u> 20 percent of the questionnaires have been returned so far.
The fund drive is still short <u>some</u> $12,000.
He was <u>some</u> 15 minutes late to the meeting that he had called!

Emphatic

This use is almost always restricted to casual, informal conversation. What is distinctive about this use is that *some* is always heavily stressed, whereas the normal uses of *some*, like all other articles, are unstressed. This use is typically used with the fixed phrase, "That was *some* . . ."

> Boy, that was *some* game last night, wasn't it?
> That was *some* party at the Brown's.
> That was *some* upset in the county election.

Jocular

This use is a form of good-natured teasing among people who know each other pretty well. It is also recognizable by a degree of stress on *some*. While this degree of stress is not as dramatic as the stress used with the emphatic form, the stress is still sufficient to distinguish this use of *some* from the normal unstressed use. The stress serves to signal the audience, "I'm only kidding." The following are some examples along with a description of the situation:

- Person A has just purchased a new flashy car. Person B, a good friend, might say, "Wow! Some people really know how to make a statement!"
- Person A has hosted a nice dinner party. One of the guests might offer the teasing compliment, "Some people really know how to live!"
- Person A is dressed unusually formally. Person B might say, "Some people really know how to dress!"

The meaning and use of *some*

The indefinite article *some* functions grammatically the same way with either a plural count noun or a noncount noun. There is a completely predictable, albeit slight, semantic difference between the two uses of *some*. When *some* modifies a plural count noun, there is more of a sense of *some* as a number word than when *some* modifies an inherently numberless noncount noun. Compare the following two sentences:

PLURAL COUNT NOUN:	John brought **some** <u>sandwiches</u>.
NONCOUNT NOUN:	Jim brought **some** <u>coffee</u>.

With the plural noun *sandwiches*, *some* is a number word meaning something like "more than one, but less than a whole lot." With the noncount noun *coffee*, *some* is not a number word at all; rather, it is more a quantity word meaning something like "a moderate amount." Whatever semantic differences there are between the two uses of *some*, the differences are completely the product of the inherent differences between the count and noncount nouns that *some* modifies.

The indefinite article *some* has an important unique feature: under certain specific conditions, we replace *some* with *any*. There is no difference in meaning between *some* and *any*: *any* functions as a de facto alternate form of the indefinite article whose use is obligatory under certain grammatical conditions. By far the most important grammatical conditions under which *any* replaces *some* are in questions and negative statements.

The following are two examples of positive statements. After the statements are the same sentence first in its question form and then in its negative statement form:

Plural count noun

STATEMENT: They attended <u>some</u> lectures on trade policy.

QUESTION: Did they attend <u>any</u> lectures on trade policy?

NEGATIVE: They didn't attend <u>any</u> lectures on trade policy.

Noncount noun

STATEMENT: Ralph did <u>some</u> homework before he went to school.

QUESTION: Did Ralph do <u>any</u> homework before he went to school?

NEGATIVE: Ralph didn't do <u>any</u> homework before he went to school.

As you can see, *any* has replaced *some* in the question and negative statement versions of the original basic sentence.

What best captures the relationship between *some* and *any* is a rule that changes *some* to *any* if and only if certain conditions are met. We will call this rule (not very imaginatively) the ***some/any* rule**. There are two versions of the *some/any* rule, one for questions and one for negative statements.

1. ***Some/any* question rule:** change *some* to *any* if *some* is inside a question.

2. ***Some/any* negative statement rule:** change *some* to *any* if *some* is inside a negative statement.

While the two versions of the *some/any* rule do exactly the same thing, the details of how and when the rules are applied are surprisingly idiosyncratic to each version. In fact, much of the rest of this section is devoted to exploring the special conditions, exceptions, and limitations unique to each version of the rule. Under some circumstances the application of the *some/any* question rule is waived—the rule isn't used at all where we would normally expect it to be applied. The application of the *some/any* negative statement rule depends entirely on how we define the term *negative*. It turns out that English defines *negative* in some surprisingly broad ways. Since the application of the *some/any* question rule and the *some/any* negative statement rule are quite different in detail, we will deal with them separately.

This section on the indefinite article *some* will conclude with an examination of three more variants of the *some/any* rule. These variants are quite different because they have nothing to do with questions and negative statements.

The *some/any* question rule

The following are some more examples of questions produced by the regular application of the *some/any* rule:

Plural count noun

STATEMENT:	There are <u>some</u> empty tables in the next room.
QUESTION:	Are there <u>any</u> empty tables in the next room?
STATEMENT:	He is watching <u>some</u> games this weekend.
QUESTION:	Is he watching <u>any</u> games this weekend?

Noncount noun

STATEMENT:	We need <u>some</u> more glue.
QUESTION:	Do we need <u>any</u> more glue?
STATEMENT:	<u>Some</u> housing will need to be replaced.
QUESTION:	Will <u>any</u> housing need to be replaced?

The rule for changing *some* to *any* in questions is completely regular in the way it works. However, under some conditions the application of the rule is waived—that is, we do not apply the rule at all; we keep the *some* in the question form of the sentence. Just for easy labeling, we will call questions that have been produced by the normal application of the *some/any* rule **any questions**. We will call questions for which the *some/any* rule has been waived **some questions**.

ANY QUESTION:	Do you have <u>any</u> questions?
SOME QUESTION:	Do you have <u>some</u> questions?

We will use a riddle to begin our discussion of the conditions under which the *some/any* question rule is waived:

Q:	When is a question not a real question?
A:	When you already know the answer.

The answer to the riddle is the key to when we waive the normal *some/any* question rule. We waive the expected application of the *some/any* rule to signal to the audience that the question we are asking is not a fully open-ended question to be taken at face value. Often *some* questions can be requests or suggestions, rather than genuine questions. For example:

Can I give you <u>some</u> advice?

The speaker is not really asking for permission to tell the audience something. This is not a real question, because the speaker already knows the answer. The speaker is going to give advice to the audience whether the audience wants to hear the advice or not. Essentially, not applying the *some/any* rule to questions where the rule is normally expected signals the audience that the question is not to be taken literally. These questions are more like rhetorical questions than genuine requests for information.

One of the most common contexts for *some* questions is where the person asking the *some* question is actually making a request or offering something. At a restaurant, we might say this to a waiter:

> Could we get <u>some</u> more water, please?

The use of the *some* question signals that (1) we are making a polite request and (2) we anticipate a positive response to the request. In fact, if we were to apply the standard *some/any* question rule to this obvious request, the result would be ungrammatical:

> Could we get **X** <u>any</u> more water, please?

The following is another use of the *some* question at a restaurant. You have finished dinner, and the waiter comes to your table to inquire if anybody at your table would like dessert. The waiter can ask the question using either *any* or *some*:

ANY QUESTION:	Would you be interested in having <u>any</u> dessert?
SOME QUESTION:	Would you be interested in having <u>some</u> dessert?

If the waiter is at all well-trained, he or she would always use the *some* question because it implies that having dessert is the normal, expected thing to do. The *any* question implies just the opposite; it is a totally open question—some people have dessert, some people don't. (This further implies that there is no particular reason for *you* to have dessert. You might as well skip it and save the calories.) Guess which question form, the *any* question or the *some* question, sells more desserts?

Here is an example between a parent and a child. The parent can ask a question about homework with either form of question:

ANY QUESTION:	Do you have <u>any</u> homework tonight?
SOME QUESTION:	Do you have <u>some</u> homework tonight?

The use of the *any* question implies that the parent genuinely does not know if the child has homework or not. In other words, the *any* question is neutral. The use of the *some* question, on the other hand, has a definite bias: the parent expects a "Yes" answer. If instead the child says, 'No," then the parent is likely to want further confirmation.

Using the *some/any* question rule *All of the following questions contain a choice between* any *and* some. *Assume that the correct answer is* any *unless there is a reason to use* some, *and choose the more appropriate answer. Two examples are provided.*

Did we get *any / ~~some~~* mail today?

Can you pick up *~~any~~ / some* milk on your way home tonight?

1. Does anybody have *any /some* information on road conditions?

2. Can I ask you *any / some* questions about the presentation?

3. Have you heard *any / some* news about the election?

4. Can I pass you *any / some* of these excellent rolls?

5. Were there *any / some* witnesses to the accident?

6. Do they have *any / some* children?

7. Have you heard of *any / some* research in this area?

8. Could we get *any / some* sales brochures for the new development?

9. Have you and your wife been playing *any / some* bridge lately?

10. Could you reserve *any / some* rooms for us on the 16th and 17th?

The *some/any* negative statement rule

The indefinite article *some* changes to *any* in negative statements. Compare the following pairs of positive and negative sentences:

Plural count noun
POSITIVE: There are <u>some</u> flights that leave before seven.
NEGATIVE: There **aren't** <u>any</u> flights that leave before seven.

Noncount noun
POSITIVE: I got <u>some</u> dirt on the lens.
NEGATIVE: I **didn't** get <u>any</u> dirt on the lens.

As you can see, in the negative statement version of the *some/any* rule, the plural indefinite article *some* in a positive sentence changes to its counterpart *any* in the negative version of the same sentence. The application of the *some/any* rule in negative statements is actually perfectly regular (unlike the application of the *some/any* rule in questions, which is waived in certain cases). The only complication using the *some/any* rule in negative statements is determining what exactly makes a negative statement negative.

Obviously, as in the case of the earlier two example sentences, we can make sentences negative by using the negative grammatical markers *not* and *no*. However, the *some/any* negative statement rule accepts other ways of making sentences "negative" besides the formal grammatical way with *not* or *no*. No less than five different ways of being negative trigger the application of the *some/any* negative statement rule. One uses negative grammatical markers, and the others use semantically negative parts of speech.

Negative grammatical markers: *not*, *no*

The use of *not* with verbs is by far the most common way of forming negative sentences. Notice that the *some/any* negative sentence rule holds equally for all the varieties of ways that *not* is attached to verbs.

Plural count nouns

POSITIVE: The kids want <u>some</u> dessert.
NEGATIVE: The kids **don't** want <u>any</u> dessert.
POSITIVE: The unit is receiving <u>some</u> signals.
NEGATIVE: The unit **isn't** receiving <u>any</u> signals.
POSITIVE: We have planted <u>some</u> new varieties of flowers this year.
NEGATIVE: We **haven't** planted <u>any</u> new varieties of flowers this year.

Noncount nouns

POSITIVE: We put <u>some</u> furniture into storage.
NEGATIVE: We **didn't** put <u>any</u> furniture into storage after all.
POSITIVE: The children may have had <u>some</u> milk at lunch.
NEGATIVE: The children might **not** have had <u>any</u> milk at lunch.
POSITIVE: We need to take <u>some</u> more time on this.
NEGATIVE: We **don't** need to take <u>any</u> more time on this.

No is not nearly so commonly used as *not*. *No* is primarily used with predicate nouns:

Plural count nouns

POSITIVE: There are reasons for <u>some</u> revisions to the plans.
NEGATIVE: There are **no** reasons for <u>any</u> revisions to the plans.
POSITIVE: There are plans for <u>some</u> ceremonies marking the anniversary.
NEGATIVE: There are **no** plans for <u>any</u> ceremonies marking the anniversary.

Noncount nouns

POSITIVE: There is hope for <u>some</u> rain soon.
NEGATIVE: There is **no** hope for <u>any</u> rain soon.
POSITIVE: There is reason for <u>some</u> optimism.
NEGATIVE: There is **no** reason for <u>any</u> optimism.

Semantically negative adverbs

The use of semantically negative adverbs such as *hardly*, *hardly ever*, *never*, *rarely*, and *seldom* is another way of forming negative sentences. The *some/any* negative sentence rule holds for the use of these adverbs.

Plural count nouns

POSITIVE: We often cut <u>some</u> flowers for decoration.
NEGATIVE: We **rarely** cut <u>any</u> flowers for decoration.
POSITIVE: He always has <u>some</u> good suggestions for us.
NEGATIVE: He **never** has <u>any</u> good suggestions for us.

Noncount nouns

POSITIVE: I usually do <u>some</u> shopping on my way home from work.
NEGATIVE: I **seldom** do <u>any</u> shopping on my way home from work.
POSITIVE: We frequently take <u>some</u> time to chat with the neighbors.
NEGATIVE: We **hardly ever** take <u>any</u> time to chat with the neighbors.

Semantically negative preposition: *without*

The preposition *without* is used to create a semantically negative adverbial prepositional phrase that functions very much like the earlier semantically negative adverbs.

Plural count nouns

POSITIVE: They approved the proposal with <u>some</u> changes.
NEGATIVE: They approved the proposal **without** <u>any</u> changes.
POSITIVE: The manuscript was printed with <u>some</u> corrections.
NEGATIVE: The manuscript was printed **without** <u>any</u> corrections.

Noncount nouns

POSITIVE: The kids cleaned up the yard with <u>some</u> help.
NEGATIVE: The kids cleaned up the yard **without** <u>any</u> help.
POSITIVE: They closed the plant with <u>some</u> attempt to relocate the staff.
NEGATIVE: The closed the plant **without** <u>any</u> attempt to relocate the staff.

Semantically negative verbs

The verbs *deny*, *discourage*, *downplay*, *refute*, and *reject* are semantically negative verbs that follow the *some/any* negative statement rule:

Plural count nouns

POSITIVE: The CEO emphasized <u>some</u> positive forecasts.
NEGATIVE: The CEO **downplayed** <u>any</u> negative forecasts.
POSITIVE: They admitted making <u>some</u> payments to government officials.
NEGATIVE: They **rejected** making <u>any</u> payments to government officials.

Noncount nouns

POSITIVE: The fertilizer encouraged <u>some</u> new growth.

NEGATIVE: The pesticide **discouraged** <u>any</u> new growth.

POSITIVE: He admitted having <u>some</u> involvement with criminal elements.

NEGATIVE: He **denied** having <u>any</u> involvement with criminal elements.

Semantically negative predicate adjectives

The adjectives *adverse to, hesitant about, reluctant to, unhappy about*, and *unwilling to* are semantically negative predicate adjectives that also follow the *some/any* negative statement rule:

Plural count nouns

POSITIVE: They were willing to discuss <u>some</u> contract changes.

NEGATIVE: They were **unwilling to** discuss <u>any</u> contract changes.

POSITIVE: I was OK with <u>some</u> unavoidable delays.

NEGATIVE: I was quite **unhappy about** <u>any</u> further delays.

Noncount nouns

POSITIVE: We were happy to engage in <u>some</u> joint ventures with them.

NEGATIVE: We were **reluctant** to engage in <u>any</u> joint ventures with them.

POSITIVE: The company was willing to share <u>some</u> technical information.

NEGATIVE: The company was **adverse to** sharing <u>any</u> technical information.

Double negatives

As an interesting aside before leaving the topic of the *some/any* negative statement rule, look at what happens to *some* and *any* when we use what is called a "double negative." A double negative results when we use a negative marker to modify an already existing negative marker. The usual result is that the two negatives cancel each other out so that the new statement ends up positive:

He is **not unhappy**. = He is happy.
I do **not disagree**. = I agree.

Now turn to the last example of a negative statement using noncount nouns in a double negative. The following is the original negative statement and a double negative version of the same sentence:

The company was **adverse to** sharing <u>any</u> technical information.
The company was **not adverse to** sharing <u>some</u> technical information.

Notice that *any* in the original negative sentence has changed back to *some* in the double negative sentence. The two negatives have cancelled each other out, turning the resulting double negative sentence into a semantically positive sentence. Thus *some* is now more appropriate than *any*.

Using the *some/any* negative statement rule *All of the following sentences contain an underlined indefinite pronoun, either* some *or* any. *Indicate if the indefinite pronoun is used incorrectly according to the* some/any *negative statement rule, and supply the correct indefinite pronoun. If the indefinite pronoun is used correctly, indicate that the sentence is OK. Two examples are given.*

The soup was better without ~~some~~ extra salt.   *any*

The traffic this morning had <u>some</u> huge delays.   OK

1. Senator Blather is totally opposed to <u>some</u> softness on crime. _____

2. Everyone denied having <u>some</u> involvement in the failed project. _____

3. There is no thought about quitting <u>some</u> time soon. _____

4. There are <u>some</u> good reasons for doing what we did. _____

5. I rarely have <u>some</u> time to myself since the baby has come. _____

6. Politicians always minimize the importance of <u>some</u> bad news. _____

7. Do you think you could do this job without <u>any</u> help? _____

8. We hardly ever see <u>some</u> of our friends lately. _____

9. We didn't get <u>some</u> pizza like we planned to. _____

10. I am averse to taking on <u>some</u> new risks at this time. _____

Other *some/any* rules

There are three remaining grammatical constructions that can also trigger the application of the *some/any* rule. Rather surprisingly, these three constructions have nothing to do with questions or negative statements, which are constructions that we normally consider to be intrinsically linked to the *some/any* rule. Moreover, these three constructions do not appear to share any common feature with each other. The three constructions are the following:

1. *some/any* adverbial *if* clause rule

2. *some/any* adverbial *before* clause rule

3. *some/any too* predicate adjective rule

We will discuss each of these three variations of the *some/any* rule in detail, and give more examples.

Some/any adverbial *if* clause rule

Dependent or subordinate adverbial clauses beginning with *if* trigger the application of the *some/any* rule. Just to see what these clauses look like, here are some sentences containing adverbial *if* clauses:

> We may cancel the picnic if it starts to rain.
> Tell me if you are getting tired.
> I will go to the game if I can get any tickets at this late date.

Inside an adverbial *if* clause, the indefinite article *some* changes to *any*. The first sentence in each of the following pairs of examples does not contain an *if* clause; the second sentence of the pair does. Note that where the first sentence has the indefinite article *some*, the *if* clause in the second sentence has *any*.

Plural count nouns

No *if* clause:	There are some problems with the program.
If clause:	Let me know **if** there are any problems with the program.
No *if* clause:	The schedule has some errors in it.
If clause:	I'm sure we will find out **if** the schedule has any errors in it.
No *if* clause:	We can locate some qualified candidates.
If clause:	Our company is hiring **if** we can locate any qualified candidates.

Noncount nouns

No *if* clause:	You may get some negative feedback.
If clause:	Check with me **if** you get any negative feedback.
No *if* clause:	The team is making some progress.
If clause:	Let me know **if** the team is making any progress.
No *if* clause:	I have to do some shopping.
If clause:	I'll be late **if** I have to do any shopping.

One of the distinctive characteristic features of adverbial *if* clauses is that we can readily move them from their normal position following the main clause to a position at the beginning of the sentence. (This process is called **inversion**.) It makes no difference to the *some/any* rule whether the adverbial *if* clause is in its normal position or in the inverted position. The following are some examples of adverbial *if* clauses with the adverbial clause first in its normal position and then in its inverted position:

NORMAL:	Be sure to call me **if** you need any help.
INVERTED:	**If** you need any help, be sure to call me.
NORMAL:	Call your lawyer **if** you have any concerns about the settlement.
INVERTED:	**If** you have any concerns about the settlement, call your lawyer.
NORMAL:	Let me know **if** you see any patio furniture you like.
INVERTED:	**If** you see any patio furniture you like, let me know.

Note: Study the use of commas in the inverted sentences. The rule is that if an adverb clause follows the main clause, no comma is used. However, if the adverb clause is inverted, it *must* be set off from the main clause with a comma.

Some/any adverbial *before* clause rule

This rule is much like the earlier adverbial *if* clause rule. An adverbial clause beginning with *before* triggers the *some/any* rule. Before looking at the *some/any* rule in detail, consider the following examples of what adverbial *before* clauses look like:

> Let's head for home **before** it starts to rain.
> I had already heard the news **before** I got to the office.
> We looked at dozens of cars **before** we found one we liked.

As we would expect, adverbial *before* clauses, like adverbial *if* clauses, can easily be inverted in front of the main clause:

> **Before** it starts to rain, let's head for home.
> **Before** I got to the office, I had already heard the news.
> **Before** we found one we liked, we looked at dozens of cars.

Inside adverbial *before* clauses, the indefinite article *some* changes to *any*. The first sentence in each pair of examples does not contain a *before* adverbial clause; the second sentence of the pair does. Note that where the first sentence has the indefinite article *some*, the *before* clause in the second sentence has *any*.

Plural count noun

No *before* clause:	We found some cars we liked.
Before clause:	We looked at dozens **before** we found any cars we liked.
No *before* clause:	Some parents drop their children off.
Before clause:	**Before** any parents drop their children off, they must sign in at the office.
No *before* clause:	There were some downed trees on the roads.
Before clause:	We were safely at home **before** there were any downed trees on the roads.
No *before* clause:	Some weeds have already sprouted.
Before clause:	We put on pre-emergence killer **before** any weeds sprouted.

Noncount nouns

No *before* clause:	We moved some furniture.
Before clause:	We protected the floor **before** we moved any furniture.
No *before* clause:	Some radiation was released into the air.
Before clause:	They closed the facility **before** any radiation was released into the air.
No *before* clause:	The police had some evidence.
Before clause:	The police knew who had committed the crime **before** they had any evidence.

| No *before* clause: | They put <u>some</u> glass back into the window frames. |
| *Before* clause: | They replaced the window frames **before** they put <u>any</u> glass back. |

It makes no difference whether the *before* clause is in its normal or inverted position; *some* still changes to *any* in either case:

Plural count noun

| NORMAL ORDER: | We talked to our lawyer **before** we filed <u>any</u> documents. |
| INVERTED ORDER: | **Before** we filed any documents, we talked to our lawyer. |

Noncount noun

| NORMAL ORDER: | I made the sauce **before** I cooked <u>any</u> pasta. |
| INVERTED ORDER: | **Before** I cooked <u>any</u> pasta, I made the sauce. |

Some/any too predicate adjective rule

When it modifies a predicate adjective, the adverb *too* triggers the *some/any* rule. Compare the use of *some* and *any* in the following dialogue:

| PERSON A: | Let's get <u>some</u> election results. |
| PERSON B: | It's **too early** to get <u>any</u> results yet. |

The use of both *some* and *any* in this dialogue are determined by the grammar of the sentences they are in. Switching the two articles would result in ungrammatical sentences:

| PERSON A: | Let's get **X** <u>any</u> election results. |
| PERSON B: | It's **too early** to get **X** <u>some</u> results yet. |

This *too* predicate adjective construction is used in two slightly different ways. In one way, the predicate adjective is followed by a verb in the infinitive form. The following are more examples of this type, with the infinitives in italics:

Plural count nouns
Our cat is **too lazy** *to catch* <u>any</u> mice.
It is **too cloudy** *to see* <u>any</u> stars tonight.
It is **too late** *to reschedule* <u>any</u> of the appointments.
Senator Blather is **too upset** *to talk* to <u>any</u> reporters right now.

Noncount nouns
I am **too tired** *to start* <u>any</u> homework now.
It is **too slippery** *to remove* <u>any</u> snow from the roof.
The kids are **too busy** *to do* <u>any</u> shopping until Saturday.

The other common way of using this construction is to use a prepositional phrase beginning with *for* after the predicate adjective. The following are some examples of this form with the preposition *for* in italics:

Plural count nouns

It is **too late** in the season *for* any more trips into the mountains.
The movie is **too upsetting** *for* any children under 10.
The house is way **too costly** *for* any buyers in this town.
The piano is **too wide** *for* any of the doorways.

Noncount nouns

It is **too hot** *for* any more outside work.
He is still **too sick** *for* any solid food.
It is **too early** in the season *for* any really cold weather.

The two ways of using the *too* predicate adjective rule are not mutually exclusive. In fact, they are often combined, especially when the subject is a generic *it* rather than a specific person or thing.

Plural count noun

PREDICATE ADJECTIVE FOLLOWED BY AN INFINITIVE:	It was **too windy** *to play* any games outside.
PREDICATE ADJECTIVE FOLLOWED BY *FOR* PREPOSITIONAL PHRASE:	It was **too windy** *for* any games outside.
PREDICATE ADJECTIVE FOLLOWED BY *FOR* PREPOSITIONAL PHRASE + AN INFINITIVE:	It was **too windy** *for* the kids *to play* any games outside.

Noncount noun

PREDICATE ADJECTIVE FOLLOWED BY AN INFINITIVE:	It was **too dark** *to do* any more painting.
PREDICATE ADJECTIVE FOLLOWED BY *FOR* PREPOSITIONAL PHRASE:	It was **too dark** *for* any more painting.
PREDICATE ADJECTIVE FOLLOWED BY *FOR* PREPOSITIONAL PHRASE + AN INFINITIVE:	It was **too dark** *for* the workers *to do* any more painting.

EXERCISE

4·3

Using the *some/any* rule in adverbial and predicate adjective constructions *All of the uses of any in the following questions are correct. Indicate which of the following three rules governs the correct use of any in each question: (a) some/any adverbial* if *clause rule, (b) some/any adverbial* before *clause rule, or (c) some/any too predicate adjective rule. Three examples are provided.*

Let me know if I get <u>any</u> replies to our memo.

(a) some/any *adverbial* if *clause rule*

Fortunately, we got paid before <u>any</u> bills were due.

(b) some/any *adverbial* before *clause rule*

The waves are too rough for <u>any</u> surfers to risk.

(c) some/any too *predicate adjective rule*

1. Fortunately, we got paid before <u>any</u> bills were due.

   _____

2. He closed the meeting before <u>any</u> delegates could object.

   _____

3. His hall was too small to hold <u>any</u> large meetings in.

   _____

4. I am too busy to take on <u>any</u> additional jobs right now.

   _____

5. If you find <u>any</u> extra keys, give them to the manager.

   _____

6. Let me know if I get <u>any</u> mail.

   _____

7. Our dogs go absolutely crazy if there is <u>any</u> thunder during the night.

   _____

The indefinite article *some*　**59**

8. The breeze was too light for <u>any</u> kites.

_____

9. The china was too fragile for <u>any</u> children to use.

_____

10. They acted before they had received <u>any</u> authorization to do so.

_____

The zero article

·5·

The zero article in English is as much a real article as the zero digit in mathematics is a real number. When we choose the option of using the zero article, we are sending a specific message. We are signaling that the noun modified by the zero article is being used to make a generalization or a categorical statement about that noun.

Zero article, definite articles, and indefinite articles

Let's compare the zero article and other types of articles such as *the*:

> ∅ Conferences are an important way of keeping up on research.
> The conferences presented by this institution are usually excellent.

The zero article in the first sentence signals the audience that the plural count noun *conferences* is being used generically; that is, it is used to make a generalization or a categorical statement about the nature of **all** conferences. The use of the definite article *the* in the second sentence sends quite a different message. The definite article tells the audience that the speaker is referring to just one particular group of conferences, namely the conferences presented by this particular institution.

Now contrast the zero article with the indefinite article *some*:

> ∅ Milk contains lots of calcium.
> There is some milk in the refrigerator.

In the first sentence, the zero article used with the noncount noun *milk* tells us that the sentence is making a general statement about the nature of all milk, namely that milk as a category of food contains a high amount of calcium. In the second sentence, the use of the indefinite article *some* with *milk* tells the audience that *milk* refers to some specific container or containers of milk, which in this case can be found in the refrigerator.

The zero article has only one meaning: that the noun being modified is being used generically or categorically—not, as is typically the case with other types of articles, to refer to particular persons, places, or things. A particularly striking example of this is the nearly exclusive use of the zero article with sayings. Sayings, almost by definition, are generalizations or categorical statements. In the following list of thirty-eight commonly used sayings, all of the articles have been underlined:

∅ Beauty is in the eye of the beholder.
∅ Beauty is only skin deep.
∅ Birds of a feather flock together.
∅ Boys will be ∅ boys.
∅ Brevity is the soul of ∅ wit.
∅ Charity begins at ∅ home.
∅ Cleanliness is next to ∅ godliness.
∅ Crime doesn't pay.
∅ Discretion is the better part of ∅ valor.
∅ Familiarity breeds ∅ contempt.
∅ Fortune only knocks once.
∅ Garbage in, ∅ garbage out.
∅ Honesty is the best policy.
∅ Life is what you make of it.
∅ Lightning never strikes twice in the same place.
Make ∅ hay while the sun shines.
∅ Man does not live by ∅ bread alone.
∅ Money doesn't grow on ∅ trees.
∅ Money talks.
∅ Nature abhors a vacuum.
∅ Necessity is the mother of ∅ invention.
∅ Nothing is certain but ∅ death and ∅ taxes.
∅ Oil and ∅ water don't mix.
∅ Opportunity only knocks once.
∅ Patience is a virtue.
∅ People who live in ∅ glass houses shouldn't throw ∅ stones.
∅ Practice makes perfect.
∅ Rags to ∅ riches.
∅ Rules are made to be broken.
∅ Seeing is ∅ believing.
∅ Silence is golden.
∅ Silence means ∅ consent.
∅ Sticks and ∅ stones may break my bones, but ∅ words will never hurt me.
There is ∅ safety in ∅ numbers.
∅ Time and ∅ time wait for no man.
∅ Truth is stranger than ∅ fiction.
∅ Variety is the spice of ∅ life.
∅ Virtue is its own reward.

There are a total of seventy-four articles used in this list of sayings. The subject of every single sentence is modified by a zero article. Most of the non-subject nouns are also modified by the zero article. Here are the actual number and percentage of all types of articles used in these thirty-eight sayings:

Zero article used	62 (84%)
Definite article *the* used	9 (12%)
Indefinite article *a* used	3 (4%)
Total number of articles used	74

This is obviously a very atypical sample of English because there is a very disproportionately high use of zero articles: 84%. The reason is that there is a perfect fit between the content of the sentences (sayings) and the inherent meaning of zero articles. Sayings by their very nature are used to make generalizations and categorical statements about the world. And as we saw earlier, the sole function of the zero article is to make generalizations and categorical statements.

When a noun is used without any article, it is sometimes hard to recognize an actual invisible article (the zero article) is being used to make a generalization or a categorical statement. Two clues help us recognize the presence of a zero article in the sentence:

1. The use of the present tense

2. The use of adverbs of frequency.

Present-tense forms

Sentences that make a generalization are usually in a present-tense form, either the simple present, the present progressive, or the present perfect. In the following examples, the noun being used to make a generalization is underlined and the present-tense verb is in italics:

Count noun

PRESENT:	∅ <u>Airports</u> *seem* impossibly crowded these days.
PRESENT PROGRESSIVE:	∅ <u>Airports</u> *are getting* more crowded every day.
PRESENT PERFECT:	∅ <u>Airports</u> *have become* way too crowded.

Noncount noun

PRESENT:	∅ <u>Flying</u> *is* more difficult every day.
PRESENT PROGRESSIVE:	∅ <u>Flying</u> *is getting* more difficult every day.
PRESENT PERFECT:	∅ <u>Flying</u> *has become* more difficult every day.

If you look back at the list of sayings, you will see that with one apparent exception, every one of them that has a verb is in a present-tense form. The following is an exception:

People who live in glass houses <u>shouldn't</u> throw stones.

The modal verb *shouldn't* is in a present-tense form, but it is actually functioning as a present-tense subjunctive.

Adverbs of frequency

Sentences that make generalizations often contain adverbs of frequency (examples of adverbs of frequency are *always, often, generally, frequently, usually,* or the negative adverb *never*). In the following sentences, the noun being used to make a generalization is underlined and the adverb of frequency is in italics:

Plural count noun
⊘ <u>Rainstorms</u> *always* come in from the south.
⊘ <u>Sweet apples</u> *never* make very good pies.
⊘ <u>Dogs</u> are *usually* quite protective of their territory.
⊘ <u>American television programs</u> *often* use laugh tracks.

Noncount noun
⊘ <u>Conflict</u> *always* has the potential to get out of hand.
⊘ <u>Wood</u> is *usually* more expensive than <u>plastic</u>.
⊘ <u>Miscommunication</u> *frequently* results in ⊘ <u>misunderstanding</u>.
⊘ <u>Sunshine</u> *generally* gets rid of moldy patches.

EXERCISE 5·1

Using the zero article for generalizations *Use the appropriate article in the blank spaces in the following sentences. If the sentence is making a generalization, use the zero article (⊘). If the sentence is not making a generalization, use the appropriate article. Two examples are provided.*

<u>⊘</u> olives are usually too salty for me.

I need to get <u>some</u> olives when I go shopping.

1. _____ Western movies have horse chases rather than car chases.

2. All too often, _____ politicians just tell people what they want to hear.

3. We are waiting until we get back all _____ replies to our request.

4. We only order _____ supplies when we run out.

5. _____ trucks are never allowed in the left lane.

6. We are required to have 1,000 units of _____ blood on hand at all times.

7. _____ highways are free of ice at the moment, but I am worried about

_____ bridges being slippery.

8. _____ bridges are inspected by _____ independent state agency.

9. In _____ park, _____ trees are beginning to turn green.

10. _____ trees play _____ major role in controlling

_____ excess carbon dioxide.

11. We must get _____ permission slips before every school outing.

12. At this time of year, _____ snow can cause delays.

13. I can't stand wearing _____ shoes without _____ socks.

14. In _____ hotel's formal dining room, _____ jackets and

_____ ties are required.

15. Whenever I travel overseas, _____ sleep becomes _____ big
problem for me.

EXERCISE
5·2

Filling in the missing articles in a paragraph *Fill in the blanks in the following paragraph with the appropriate articles. Use Ø for the zero article. The first is done as an example.*

Ø travel by _____ air has become everyone's favorite topic to complain about. We all have heard _____ stories about _____ passengers being stuck for hours on _____ runways and _____ stories about _____ endless lines at _____ ticket counters. These are all true. _____ problem is that none of us is willing to pay what it would cost to fix _____ problems. None of us wants to pay _____ penny more than we have to. When _____ airlines try to raise _____ prices to improve their services, we all go to _____ airlines that have not raised their prices. When _____ airports try to get approval to raise _____ taxes to pay for _____ airport improvements, we vote _____ bond issues down.

Summary of article usage

·6·

As we have seen, each of the four articles in English has its own distinct function and range of meanings. This chapter summarizes the key ideas that you need to take away from this presentation.

The definite article *the*

Use the definite article *the* if and only if *both* of the following about the noun being modified are true:

1. You (the speaker or writer) have a specific person, place, thing, or idea in mind.

2. You (the speaker or writer) can reasonably assume that the intended listener or reader will know which specific person, place, thing, or idea you mean.

The critical requirement is the second one, that the listener or reader can be reasonably assumed to know *which* noun you are referring to.

In practice, the second requirement is usually met in one of four ways.

Previous mention

Use the definite article *the* with a particular noun if you have already introduced the noun to the listener or reader, in a previous sentence:

> I came down with a cold last week. It is absolutely the worst cold I've had in years.

We use the definite article with *cold* in the second sentence because the noun *cold* was introduced in the first sentence.

Defined by modifiers

Even if a noun has not been previously mentioned, use the definite article if the noun is followed by modifiers that serve to uniquely identify it. The modifier can be a full-blown adjective (relative) clause or a short adjectival phrase—any noun modifier that is sufficiently detailed to identify the noun to the audience. The following example has the modifier in italics:

> The car *parked behind me* is a new Porsche.

Normal expectations

Use the definite article if the noun is something that we can reasonably expect from the context of the sentence even if there has been no previous mention of the noun. For example, in the following sentence,

> On our last flight, the pilot had the seat belt sign on during the whole flight.

We use the with both *pilot* and *seat belt sign* even though neither has been mentioned before because we have a normal expectation that airplanes will have *pilots* and *seat belt signs*. The category of normal expectations is widely extended with names of places that we would expect to find in certain locations. So in a city, we would use *the* with all the places we would expect to find in a city even though they have not actually been mentioned:

> the post office
> the drugstore
> the police station
> the airport
> the supermarket

Uniqueness

We use *the* with things that we already know about because they are unique. Some things are unique because they are physically or logically unique, for example, *the sun, the moon, the horizon, the earth, the north pole, the future,* and *the past*. More frequent are things that are unique in a particular context or situation. If you overheard some people listening to a game on the radio, you might ask this question:

> What's the score?

Since we know that every game has a score, there is only going to be one unique score to the game people are listening to. The noun *score* is defined by the uniqueness of that particular event.

The singular indefinite article *a/an*

The indefinite article *a/an* is inherently singular because it is derived from the number *one*. A common source of error involving *a/an* is when *a/an* is used to modify a noncount noun. Even though noncount nouns are grammatically singular as far as subject/verb agreement is concerned, noncount nouns are *semantically* numberless—they are neither singular nor plural and thus cannot be used with any number words, including the singular indefinite article *a/an*. For example, in the sentence,

> We have **X** a high respect for our mayor.

a is ungrammatical because it modifies the noncount noun *respect*.

In one respect, *a/an* is the complete opposite of *the*: *a/an* signals to the audience that the noun *a/an* modifies is new information. (*The* is just the opposite: *the* signals that the information is already known to the audience.) The most common function for *a/an* is to introduce a specific new topic to the discourse, often by changing the subject. The use of *a* in the sentence,

> We saw a really good program on television last night.

announces an intent to talk about the TV program.

We have called this use of the indefinite article a **specific indefinite article** because it introduces a specific new topic. A **nonspecific indefinite article** is more of a general comment. If a person says,

> I need a glass of water.

the person does not have a specific glass of water in mind, nor is the person introducing a glass of water as a new topic of conversation.

There are two additional uses of nonspecific indefinite articles:

1. To characterize or define someone or something as a member of a class. Many definitions use nonspecific indefinite articles:

   > An ibex is a species of wild goat.

2. To make generalizations. We use the nonspecific indefinite article to talk in general terms:

   > A good plan is easy to understand and easy to implement.

   The sentence is not talking about any actual plan, but is making a generalization about the nature of good plans.

The indefinite article *some*

Some is used with two different categories of nouns: plural count nouns and noncount nouns. When *some* is used with plural count nouns, *some* is the plural counterpart of the singular indefinite article *a/an*.

SINGULAR INDEFINITE ARTICLE:	We need to get a new map.
PLURAL INDEFINITE ARTICLE:	We need to get some new maps.

The indefinite article *some* has an important unique feature: under certain specific conditions, we replace *some* with *any*. There is no difference in meaning between *some* and *any*: *any* functions as a de facto alternate form of the indefinite article whose use is obligatory under certain grammatical conditions. By far the most important grammatical conditions under which *any* replaces *some* are in questions and negative statements (called the **some/any rule** in this book). Since the change of *some* to *any* is somewhat different in questions and negative statements, we deal with them separately.

Some/any question rule

Here are two examples of the standard application of the *some/any* question rule:

Plural count noun

STATEMENT: The audience asked <u>some</u> questions.

QUESTION: Did the audience <u>ask</u> any questions?

Noncount noun

STATEMENT: Sarah returned <u>some</u> messages before she left.

QUESTION: Did Sarah return <u>any</u> messages before she left?

The problem is that under certain conditions we waive the application of the *some/any* question rule; that is, *some* does **not** change to *any* in questions. The most common condition under which the *some/any* question rule is waived is when the person asking the question is actually making a request or offering something. In other words, the question form is not actually being used as a genuine request for information. At a restaurant, we might say the following to a waiter:

Could we get <u>some</u> more water, please?

The use of the *some* rather than the expected *any* question signals (1) that we are making a polite request, not asking a genuine question, and (2) that we anticipate a positive response to the request. In fact, if we were to apply the standard *some/any* question rule to this obvious request, the result would be ungrammatical:

Could we get **X** <u>any</u> more water, please?

Some/any negative statement rule

The indefinite article *some* changes to *any* in negative statements. Compare the following pairs of positive and negative sentences:

Plural count noun

POSITIVE: There are <u>some</u> pencils on the front desk.

NEGATIVE: There **aren't** <u>any</u> pencils on the front desk.

Noncount noun

POSITIVE: Our new floor needs <u>some</u> protection until it dries.

NEGATIVE: The floor **doesn't** need <u>any</u> protection now.

As you can see, in the negative statement version of the *some/any* rule, the plural indefinite article *some* in a positive sentence changes to its counterpart *any* in the negative version of the same sentence.

The difficulty with applying the *some/any* negative statement rule is recognizing the surprisingly diverse variety of grammatical constructions that trigger the application of the *some/any* negative statement rule. There are no less than eight different triggers for the application of the rule. Some of these triggers are obvious, some make a little sense, and some are quite puzzling. The following, listed in rough approximation of predictability, are the eight triggers for the *some/any* negative statement rule:

1. Negative grammatical markers: *not, no*

Plural count noun

POSITIVE: I saw <u>some</u> parking places in the back.

NEGATIVE: I **didn't** <u>see</u> any parking places in the back.

Noncount noun

POSITIVE: They need <u>some</u> assistance.

NEGATIVE: They **don't** need any assistance.

2. Semantically negative adverbs: *hardly, hardly ever, never, rarely, seldom*

Plural count noun

POSITIVE: The gardeners often save <u>some</u> seeds for next year.

NEGATIVE: The gardeners **hardly ever** save <u>any</u> seeds for next year.

Noncount noun

POSITIVE: There was <u>some</u> confusion about the layoffs.

NEGATIVE: There was **never** <u>any</u> confusion about the layoffs.

3. Semantically negative preposition: *without*

Plural count noun

POSITIVE: The attack took place with <u>some</u> losses.

NEGATIVE: The attack took place **without** <u>any</u> losses.

Noncount noun

POSITIVE: The transition occurred with <u>some</u> confusion.

NEGATIVE: The transition occurred **without** <u>any</u> confusion.

4. Semantically negative verbs: *deny, discourage, downplay, refute,* and *reject*

> **Plural count noun**
> POSITIVE: Senator Blather admitted <u>some</u> lapses in judgment.
> NEGATIVE: Senator Blather **denied** making <u>any</u> lapses in judgment.

> **Noncount noun**
> POSITIVE: He also admitted using <u>some</u> campaign money inappropriately.
> NEGATIVE: He also **rejected** using <u>any</u> campaign money inappropriately.

5. Semantically negative predicate adjectives: *adverse to, hesitant about, reluctant to, unhappy about,* and *unwilling to*

> **Plural count noun**
> POSITIVE: They were agreeable to <u>some</u> of the proposed changes.
> NEGATIVE: They were **adverse to** <u>any</u> of the proposed changes.

> **Noncount noun**
> POSITIVE: I was willing to reveal <u>some</u> information.
> NEGATIVE: I was **hesitant about** revealing <u>any</u> private information.

6. Adverbial *if* clauses

> **Plural count noun**
> No *if* clause: Let's watch <u>some</u> television.
> *If* clause: We would have more time **if** we didn't watch <u>any</u> television.

> **Noncount noun**
> No *if* clause: We are getting <u>some</u> criticism.
> *If* clause: Let me know **if** we are getting <u>any</u> criticism.

7. Adverbial *before* clause

> **Plural count noun**
> No *before* clause: We made <u>some</u> important decisions.
> *Before* clause: We need to talk **before** we make <u>any</u> important decisions.

> **Noncount noun**
> No *before* clause: The police can only act when they have <u>some</u> real evidence.
> *Before* clause: The police acted **before** they had <u>any</u> real evidence.

8. *too* predicate adjective

Plural count noun

No *too* predicate adjective: The announcement had <u>some</u> impact on the election.

Too predicate adjective: The announcement was **too late** to have <u>any</u> impact on the election.

Noncount noun

No *too* predicate adjective: Let's do <u>some</u> more work.

Too predicate adjective: We were **too upset** to do <u>any</u> more work.

The zero article, ∅

When we choose the option of using the zero article, we are sending a specific message. We are signaling that the noun the zero article modifies is being used to make a generalization or a categorical statement. Here is a famous line from President Roosevelt's First Inaugural Address in 1933:

> The only thing we have to fear is ∅ fear itself.

The noun *fear* is usually used as a count noun, but in this quote the use of the zero article tells us that the noun *fear* is being used as an abstract category. Roosevelt very skillfully uses the zero article to personify fear as an actual malevolent entity in its own right that we must fight.

Two clues help us recognize the presence of a zero article in the sentence: the use of the present tense and the use of adverbs of frequency.

Present-tense forms

Sentences that make generalizations are usually in a present-tense form, either the simple present, the present progressive, or the present perfect. In the following examples, the noun being used to make a generalization is underlined, and the present-tense verb is in italics:

Count noun

PRESENT: ∅ <u>Airports</u> *seem* impossibly crowded these days.

PRESENT PROGRESSIVE: ∅ <u>Airports</u> *are getting* more crowded every day.

PRESENT PERFECT: ∅ <u>Airports</u> *have become* way too crowded.

Noncount noun

PRESENT: ∅ <u>Flying</u> *is* more difficult every day.

PRESENT PROGRESSIVE: ∅ <u>Flying</u> *is getting* more difficult every day.

PRESENT PERFECT: ∅ <u>Flying</u> *has become* more difficult every day.

Adverb of frequency

Sentences that make generalizations often contain adverbs of frequency (e.g., *always, often, generally, frequently, usually,* or the negative adverb *never*). In the following sentences, the noun being used to make a generalization is underlined and the adverb of frequency is in italics:

Plural count noun

∅ Rainstorms *always* come in from the south.

∅ Sweet apples *never* make very good pies.

∅ Dogs are *usually* quite protective of their territory.

∅ American television programs *often* use laugh tracks.

Noncount noun

∅ Conflict *always* has the potential to get out of hand.

∅ Wood is *usually* more expensive than ∅ plastic.

∅ Miscommunication *frequently* results in ∅ misunderstanding.

∅ Sunshine *generally* gets rid of moldy patches.

Now that you have reviewed the four categories of articles—the definite article *the*, the indefinite article *a/an*, *some/any*, and the zero article—you can refer back to this chapter when you need to refresh the key points.

DETERMINERS

·7· An introduction to determiners

In this section we will look in detail at the use and meanings of the more common and important determiners with a special emphasis on those determiners that cause trouble for nonnative speakers (and oftentimes for native speakers as well).

The term **determiner** is used in two slightly different ways. In formal grammatical studies, *determiner* is used broadly to include the entire class of pre-adjective noun modifiers (including the articles *the* and *a/an*). In English language textbooks, *determiner* is usually used more narrowly to refer to all determiners *except for* the articles *the* and *a/an* (and sometimes *some*). There is no real conflict between these definitions: articles are, in fact, a subclass of determiners. Textbooks (quite reasonably) separate out articles from the other determiners for a practical pedagogical reason: articles require much more extensive treatment than the other determiners.

Let us begin by defining what determiners are (defining *determiner* here in the broader sense that includes articles). Determiners are a special group of pre-adjective noun modifiers. Determiners are adjectives only in the widest sense that determiners, like adjectives, also modify nouns. Determiners differ from what we will now call "true adjectives" both **semantically** and **grammatically**.

Semantically, there is a basic difference in meaning between determiners and true adjectives. True adjectives describe some characteristic or property of the particular nouns they modify, but determiners do not. All determiners have the function of helping the audience (the listener or reader) determine *which* noun the speaker is referring to. In fact, this is where the meaning of the grammatical term *determiner* comes from: determiners help "determine" which particular noun a speaker or author means. Compare the true adjective *large* and the determiner *these* in the following sentence:

We need to move <u>these</u> <u>large</u> boxes into the hall.

In this sentence, the true adjective *large* is used to describe a property or characteristic of the noun *boxes*—their physical size. However, the determiner *these* does not describe any property physically inherent in these boxes. There is no property of "these-ness" that these boxes themselves possess. The function of the determiner *these* is to help the listener identify which particular set of boxes the speaker is talking about. *These* identifies the boxes as being the ones nearer the speaker (as opposed to *those* boxes—the ones farther away from the speaker).

Note: the determiner *these* locates the boxes in space at this particular moment in time. It really has nothing to do with the intrinsic nature of the boxes at all, only where they happen to be at the moment in reference to the speaker and audience. For example:

> We finally found <u>a</u> <u>good</u> dentist.

The adjective *good* describes a property or quality the speaker attributes to the speaker's dentist, the quality of being *good*. The determiner *a* does not attribute any comparable property to the dentist. It does, however, give us a very different kind of information: it tells us that the speaker of the sentence does not expect us, the audience, to already know the particular dentist the speaker is talking or writing about. This information (unlike the information contained in the adjective *good*) has absolutely nothing to do with any characteristic or property inherent in the speaker's dentist. The use of *a* has everything to do with the relationship and state of knowledge between the speaker and the audience and very little to do with the inherent nature of dentists.

As we have seen from these two examples, determiners are a kind of contextual aid that speakers or writers use to help their audience tell *which* particular noun or nouns they are referring to at the moment. True adjectives, on the other hand, are like descriptive tags that speakers or writers attach to particular nouns and which last for the duration of that particular language event.

EXERCISE

7·1

Distinguishing determiners from true adjectives by meaning

*The following sentences contain one or more underlined noun modifiers. For each underlined noun, decide only on the basis of meaning whether (a) the modifier is a **determiner** that helps the reader identify which noun the writer is referring to or (b) the modifier is a **true adjective** that describes some aspect or feature of the noun itself. Two examples are provided.*

Fortunately, we took <u>more</u> food than we absolutely needed. *determiner*

We always try to eat <u>fresh</u> fruit for breakfast. *true adjective*

1. He has to keep <u>accurate</u> records of all the expenses. _____

2. Sit at <u>whatever</u> table you want. _____

3. They stayed at our house over spring break. _____

4. The play was a tremendous success. _____

5. Some people had to leave early. _____

6. The thick drapes kept the room dark and surprisingly warm. _____

7. Every day is a completely new challenge. _____

8. Two people were waiting outside the office. _____

9. The warm weather was making me sleepy. _____

10. I felt a sharp pain in my knees. _____

Grammatically, there are three formal differences between determiners and true adjectives: (1) comparative and superlative forms, (2) ability to function as pronouns, and (3) word order.

Comparative and superlative forms

The vast majority of true adjectives have comparative and superlative forms: some formed with -er and -est, others formed with more and most.

TRUE ADJECTIVE	COMPARATIVE	SUPERLATIVE
direct	more direct	most direct
blue	bluer	bluest
needy	more needy	most needy
tall	taller	tallest
certain	more certain	most certain
soft	softer	softest
scholarly	more scholarly	most scholarly

Determiners do not have comparative or superlative forms. Attempts to make them comparative or superlative produce ludicrous results:

DETERMINER	COMPARATIVE	SUPERLATIVE
both	X bother	X bothest
	X more both	X most both
first	X firster	X firstest
	X more first	X most first
that	X thater	X thatest
	X more that	X most that

DETERMINER	COMPARATIVE	SUPERLATIVE
half	**X** halfer	**X** halfest
	X more half	**X** most half
his	**X** hiser	**X** hisest
	X more his	**X** most his

Distinguishing true adjectives from determiners by using comparative and superlative forms *Identify which of the following underlined noun modifiers are true adjectives and which are determiners. Confirm your answers by putting the underlined adjectives into the comparative and superlative forms. The true adjectives will make grammatical comparative and superlative forms, but the determiners will not. Two examples are provided.*

The storm brought with it <u>wild</u> winds.

wild—*true adjective: comparative:* wilder; *superlative:* wildest

<u>Both</u> sides have agreed to binding arbitration.

Both—*determiner: comparative:* **X** both-er; *superlative:* **X** both-est

1. We were delighted by our <u>unexpected</u> award.

   _____

2. I liked it so much I had a <u>double</u> helping.

   _____

3. I finally passed my <u>last</u> qualifying test.

   _____

4. We began a <u>rapid</u> descent down the icy path.

   _____

5. <u>Neither</u> candidate had enough votes to win outright.

   _____

6. We got an <u>enthusiastic</u> approval for our revised plans.

   _____

7. <u>That</u> coffee is not very good.

   _____

8. I washed all the <u>dirty</u> dishes that were stacked up in the kitchen.

_____

9. There was an <u>amazing</u> rumor going around the office this morning.

_____

10. They had <u>enough</u> money to rent a better apartment.

_____

Ability to function as pronouns

Determiners have an unusual characteristic: most of them can be turned into pronouns that replace the nouns that the determiners modify. In the sentence,

> I thought the <u>last</u> question was the hardest one.

the determiner *last* can be used as a pronoun replacing the noun *question* that it modifies:

> I thought the <u>last</u> ~~question~~ was the hardest.

Note that the information contained in the noun being modified is totally lost in the process. In other words, a pronoun derived from a determiner requires the listener to know from context what that newly created pronoun refers to, because the noun it modified has been deleted from the new sentence. As you might expect, this construction is primarily used in casual conversation where the listener can easily fill in what is missing in the language of the sentence.

Here are some more examples with the underlined determiner in the first of the pair playing the role of a pronoun in the second of the pair:

> <u>Neither</u> one has lived here long. (modifier)
> <u>Neither</u> has lived here long. (pronoun)
> Take <u>any</u> bicycle that you want. (modifier)
> Take <u>any</u> that you want. (pronoun)
> <u>Many</u> people are called, but <u>few</u> people are chosen. (modifier)
> <u>Many</u> are called, but <u>few</u> are chosen. (pronoun)
> <u>Which</u> jacket do you like the best? (modifier)
> <u>Which</u> do you like the best? (pronoun)
> Everyone wants to get one of <u>those</u> new iPads. (modifier)
> Everyone wants to get one of <u>those</u>. (pronoun)

Note that in the last example, the pronoun *those* replaces not only the noun *iPads*, but also the modifying adjective *new*.

Turning determiners into pronouns *Each of the following sentences contains an underlined determiner. Turn the determiners into pronouns; then make the necessary deletions or changes. An example is provided.*

Do you have <u>enough</u> money?

Do you have enough?

1. It is hard when <u>both</u> children are out of school at the same time.

_____

2. Take <u>whichever</u> seat you want.

_____

3. <u>Each</u> storm seems worse than the previous one.

_____

4. The audience will have <u>a few</u> questions to ask the speaker.

_____

5. They will probably accept <u>whatever</u> offer you give them.

_____

6. We couldn't decide <u>which</u> movie we wanted to see.

_____

7. Unfortunately, we had <u>little</u> time to spare.

_____

8. The <u>first</u> pancake always seems to stick to the pan.

_____

9. <u>Most</u> children in the United States go to public schools.

_____

10. <u>This</u> idea is never going to work.

_____

As we would predict, true adjectives cannot function as pronouns. In the sentence,

> We came to an <u>important</u> conclusion.

we cannot delete the noun *conclusion* and turn the true adjective *important* into a pronoun:

> **X** We came to an <u>important</u>.

What has been just presented is certainly the case for formal English; however, casual spoken English can sometimes play by a different set of rules. If the true adjective is by itself, that is, *not* preceded by an article, we can turn the true adjective into a kind of pseudo-pronoun:

> We just bought <u>new</u> chairs for the living room.

We can delete the noun *chair*, changing the true adjective *new* into the functional equivalent of a pronoun:

> We just bought **new** ~~chairs~~ for the living room.

The new pseudo-pronoun *new* now carries a primary sentence stress in place of the secondary stress that the original true adjective *new* carried. Here are some more examples of true adjectives turned into pseudo-pronouns:

> I really like <u>spicy</u> food. (adjective)
> I really like **spicy** ~~food~~. (quasi-pronoun)
> We prefer <u>red</u> wine with pasta. (adjective)
> We prefer **red** ~~wine~~ with pasta. (quasi-pronoun)
> I always buy <u>cheap</u> airline tickets when I fly domestic. (adjective)
> I always buy **cheap** ~~airline tickets~~ when I fly domestic. (quasi-pronoun)

Word order

The most important grammatical difference between determiners and true adjectives is word order: determiners must precede true adjectives. It is the most important difference because whenever there is both a determiner and an adjective modifying the same noun, the user must decide which modifiers are determiners and which are true adjectives in order to put them into their correct left-to-right order. The following are some examples with the determiners and adjectives underlined and labeled:

> Their store is located in <u>an</u> <u>expensive</u> shopping area.
>   det. adj.
> It was only <u>a</u>   <u>rough</u> estimate.
>   det. adj.
> <u>The</u> <u>massive</u> explosion was caused by a buildup of coal gas.
> det. adj.

If we try to put the two modifiers in reverse order with the adjective preceding the determiner, the result is, of course, completely ungrammatical:

    X Their store is located in <u>expensive</u> <u>an</u> shopping area.
                                            adj.   det.
    X It was only <u>rough</u> <u>a</u> estimate.
                      adj. det.
    X <u>Massive</u> <u>the</u> explosion was caused by a buildup of coal gas.
     adj.   det.

Putting determiners and true adjectives in the correct left-to-right order *Each of the following sentences contains a pair of blank spaces. At the end of each sentence are two noun modifiers—one a true adjective and one a determiner (in alphabetical order). Decide which is the true adjective and which is the determiner, and put them in the correct left-to-right order. Two examples are provided.*

She has received *several* *major* awards for her photography. <u>major</u>, <u>several</u>

There were *three* *bright* stars on the eastern horizon. <u>bright</u>, <u>three</u>

1. After _____ _____ starts, I finally got the right answer. <u>a few</u>, <u>false</u>

2. The detective noticed _____ _____ scars on the victim's face. <u>numerous</u>, <u>parallel</u>

3. _____ _____ blankets need to be cleaned. <u>those</u>, <u>woolen</u>

4. The patient was taking _____ _____ breaths. <u>many</u>, <u>shallow</u>

5. _____ _____ landscapes need more green space. <u>most</u>, <u>urban</u>

6. _____ _____ jobs pay a very good wage. <u>beginning</u>, <u>few</u>

7. _____ _____ outcome should have been anticipated. <u>poor</u>, <u>such a</u>

8. _____ _____ guess turned out to be far too low. <u>best</u>, <u>my</u>

9. We looked at _____ _____ houses over the weekend. <u>comparable</u>, <u>several</u>

10. Their program has produced _____ _____ physicians. <u>dozens of</u>, <u>local</u>

Determiners are a remarkably unruly part of speech. There is no universally accepted terminology for talking about determiners. In this book we use a broad definition of *determiner* that includes not only articles, but also entire possessive noun phrases:

> They announced the first-place winner's prize.

The key characteristic that all determiners in this book share is that we can substitute the basic determiners for them (i.e., articles, demonstratives, and possessives):

> They announced the first-place winner's prize.

They announced	the	prize. (article)
They announced	that	prize. (demonstrative)
They announced	her	prize. (possessive)

In this book we focus primarily on the meaning and use of those determiners that are most likely to cause problems for nonnative speakers (and not just a few native speakers as well).

Definite determiners

There are two main types of determiners: **definite determiners** and **quantifiers**. Definite determiners serve to specifically define the noun modified by the determiners. Quantifiers are determiners that specify the quantity or amount of the noun being modified. We will explore definite determiners first and then turn to selected quantifiers.

The prototypical definite determiner is the definite article *the*. There are three main types of definite determiners:

1. definite article *the*

2. demonstrative determiners *this*, *that*, *these*, and *those*

3. possessive determiners such as possessive pronouns (*my, our, your, his, her, its, their*), possessive nouns (*Mary's, Henry's*), and possessive noun phrases (*the school's, most of the team's*)

The use of *the* establishes that both the speaker and the audience know which specific oranges the speaker is referring to. Since *the* was discussed in great detail in Part I, it will not be discussed further in Part II.

> I want to get <u>the</u> oranges that are on sale.

Demonstrative determiners

The demonstrative determiners are *this*, *that*, *these*, and *those*. *This* and *that* are singular; *these* and *those* are plural.

SINGULAR	PLURAL
Do you like <u>this</u> hat?	Do you like <u>these</u> hats?
Do you like <u>that</u> hat?	Do you like <u>those</u> hats?

The difference between *this/these* on the one hand and *that/those* on the other is much more complicated than the simple numerical distinction between *this/these* on the one hand and *that/those* on the other. Generally speaking, *this/these* have a sense of "closeness" and *that/those* have a sense of "distance." The closeness and distance distinction can be in space, time, or emotional distance.

Space

This house [the closer of two houses] has a blue roof.

That house [the more distant of two houses] has a red roof.

I took these pictures [the closer ones], but not those pictures [the more distant ones].

Time

I was able to finish the project this week because I had more time than
I did that week [a week at some more distant time in the past].

Did you like these movies [the ones that we just saw] better than
those movies [the ones we saw earlier]?

Emotional distance

I like this new work schedule they are talking about.

I don't like that new work schedule they came up with.

I like this waiter, don't you?

That waiter really irritates me.

I am going to get some more of these delicious nuts, would you like some?

Those cheese balls are too spicy for me.

Everything else being equal, we tend to use *this* and *these* for people and things we like or feel positive about and *that* and *those* for people and things we do not like.

Previous reference

In writing, especially more formal writing, we use demonstrative determiners along with collective nouns to refer back to previous material. An example of this follows:

> Contact sports, especially where there are sharp or repeated blows to the head, may be much more dangerous than previously thought. The brains of young girls are especially susceptible to this kind of injury.

Using the demonstrative determiner *this* with an abstract collective noun like *kind* is a way of referring to and summarizing previously stated information without having to repeat the actual words.

> *those* + noun + restrictive adjective clause

We can use the demonstrative determiner *those* to specify a noun that will be further identified by information in a restrictive adjective clause that follows the noun. In effect, using *those* alerts the audience that the noun *those* modifies is going to be further defined. Here is an example of this use of *those* with the restrictive adjective clause underlined:

> Will those students who need a copy of the new schedule please see me?

This sentence would still be grammatical if we deleted the demonstrative determiner:

> Will ~~those~~ students who need a copy of the new schedule please see me?

The purpose of using *those* is to emphasize that the information given pertains *only* to the identified group, which is exactly what we would expect a demonstrative determiner to do.

> Please give me those forms that you have already completed.
> Those people who didn't get flu shots this year are taking a big risk.
> The police are interviewing all those people who saw the accident.
> Those cars that have defective airbags are being recalled.

Introduce a new topic

In informal conversation, *this* and *these* can be used to introduce a new topic. For example, in the following phrase,

> There was *this* guy at the party last night . . .

the use of *this* signals two things to the listener: (1) the speaker has a very specific person in mind but is aware that the listener does not know yet who the speaker is talking about, and (2) the speaker is introducing this person as a new topic of conversation. Accordingly, we would expect the speaker to elaborate on what was so interesting about that person. The following sentence with *these* is similar:

> Ralph's boss said that he had *these* concerns.

Again, the use of *these* signals that (1) Ralph's boss has very specific concerns in mind and (2) the concerns have now been introduced as a new topic of conversation.

Possessive determiners

Possessive determiners are possessive pronouns, possessive nouns, and possessive noun phrases that modify and define a following noun or noun phrase. In the sentence,

> I finally found my **car keys** in the back of a chair.

the possessive determiner *my* specifically defines the noun modified by the determiner. In this case, the possessive determiner tells the audience whose car keys were in the back of the chair.

Possessive pronouns

The following are some examples of each of the three grammatical types of possessive determiner:

Possessive pronouns
His **answer** came as a complete surprise.
Our **position** on this matter is perfectly clear.
We placed the TV where its **screen** was visible from everywhere in the room.

One confusing aspect about possessive pronouns is that there are two separate sets of them: one set that functions as true pronouns and a second set that functions as possessive determiners. Compare the underlined pronouns in the following pair of sentences:

PRONOUN:	Excuse me, I think that book is <u>mine</u>.
POSSESSIVE DETERMINERS:	Excuse me, I think that is <u>my</u> book.

In the first, the possessive pronoun *mine* is functioning as a true pronoun, the complement of the noun *book*. We can confirm this analysis by replacing the possessive pronoun *mine* with the personal pronoun *it*:

Excuse me, I think that book is <u>mine</u>.
<u>it</u>

In the second, the possessive determiner *my* functions as an adjective modifying the noun *book*. If we perform the same test and replace *my* with the personal pronoun *it*, the result is nonsense:

Excuse me, I think that is <u>my</u> book.
X it

The reason why the test doesn't work on this sentence is that to be grammatical the third-person pronoun *it* must replace the entire noun phrase, not just a part of it:

Excuse me, I think that is <u>my book</u>.
it

We can also easily confirm the basic differences between the possessive determiner *my* and the possessive pronoun *mine* by trying to switch them for each other:

X Excuse me, I think that is <u>mine</u> book.
X Excuse me, I think that is <u>my</u>.

Here are the complete paradigms for both sets of forms of possessives:

FIRST-PERSON POSSESSIVE	SINGULAR	PLURAL
Used as adjective	my	our
Used as pronoun	mine	ours

SECOND-PERSON POSSESSIVE		
Used as adjective	your	your
Used as pronoun	yours	yours

THIRD-PERSON POSSESSIVE		
Used as adjective	his, her, its	their
Used as pronoun	his, hers, its	theirs

You may have noticed that all of the forms of the possessive adjective and possessive pronoun are different, with two exceptions: *his* and *its*. The two uses of *his* do not pose any real problems, but the two uses of *its* can lead to confusion. In the third-person singular, referring to abstractions or other inanimate objects, the form *its* is used for both possessive determiners and possessive pronouns.

If it is important to tell which one is which, they can be distinguished by position. When used as a possessive determiner, *its* must precede the noun it modifies:

> The dog has lost its toy bone again.

When *its* is used as a possessive pronoun, *its* must occur in a position that a pronoun or noun can occupy:

> The cat's food is on the shelf; its [referring to the dog's food] is under the sink.

Its is in a noun position: *its* is the subject of the verb *is*.

However, there is a considerable usage problem distinguishing the possessive determiner *its* from *it's*, the contracted form of *it is*. You might not think that confusing these two forms would pose such a problem; after all, the contracted form is spelled differently—with an apostrophe.

The problem is that native and nonnative speakers alike associate the use of an apostrophe with possession. If the *man's*, the *person's*, the *nation's*, and the *student's* all use apostrophes and they are all possessive, it is very easy to overgeneralize and incorrectly spell the possessive determiner *its* **X** i-t-'-s to follow the same pattern. If the following sentences were part of lengthy paragraphs, do you think you would have noticed that the possessive determiners were incorrect?

> The company is thinking of changing it's advertising agency.
> I hope to submit it's final design sometime next week.
> It's a terrible disease, but no knows what it's cause is.
> The game is pretty complicated, but it's basic premise is simple enough.

Here is a very helpful way to distinguish the possessive determiner *its* from the contraction of *it is*: the **it's expansion test**. Anytime you use *it's*, check to see if *it's* really is a contraction by expanding the *it's* form back into two independent words: *it is*. The result will immediately tell you whether *it's* is the contraction of *it is* or a misspelled form of the possessive determiner *its*.

Let's apply the *it's* expansion test to the four example sentences:

> The company is thinking of changing it's advertising agency.
> *It's* expansion test: **X** The company is thinking of changing *it is* advertising agency.
> Correction: The company is thinking of changing **its** advertising
>   agency.

I hope to submit it's final design sometime next week.
It's expansion test: **X** I hope to submit ***it is*** final design sometime next week.
Correction: I hope to submit **its** final design sometime next week.

It's a terrible disease, but no one knows what it's cause is.
It's expansion test: **X** ***It is*** a terrible disease, but no one knows what **it is** cause is.
Correction: **It's** a terrible disease, but no one knows what **its** cause is.

The game is pretty complicated, but it's basic premise is simple enough.
It's expansion test: **X** The game is pretty complicated, but ***it is*** basic premise is
                                simple enough.
Correction: The game is pretty complicated, but **its** basic premise is simple
                                enough.

Note that in the third sentence, the *it's* expansion test is applied twice: the first test shows that the first *it's* is indeed a contraction of *it is*; the second application shows that the second *it's* is incorrectly used.

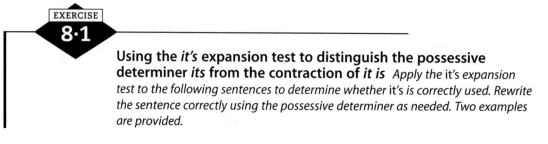

EXERCISE
8·1

Using the *it's* expansion test to distinguish the possessive determiner *its* from the contraction of *it is* Apply the it's expansion test to the following sentences to determine whether it's is correctly used. Rewrite the sentence correctly using the possessive determiner as needed. Two examples are provided.

The boat had already left **it's** berth at the dock.

its

Expansion test: **X** *The boat had already left **it is** berth at the dock.*

I can't hear them very well; **it's** a terrible connection.

Expansion test: OK *I can't hear them very well; **it is** a terrible connection.*

1. I'm afraid that **it's** a problem we have no easy solution for.

   _____

2. Like many older cities, **it's** downtown has suffered extensive decay.

   _____

3. After the bankruptcy, **it's** assets were frozen by the court.

   _____

4. **It's** a solution in search of a problem.

_____

5. I must say, **it's** architecture came as an absolute surprise.

_____

6. Fortunately, **it's** limitations are well known.

_____

7. The movie was very affecting; **it's** final scenes were really moving.

_____

8. **It's** a controversy that never seems to end.

_____

9. We have been discussing **it's** surprising success.

_____

10. The facility has totally outgrown **it's** maximum capacity.

_____

Possessive nouns

These are stand-alone nouns without any kind of modifiers (because if the nouns have modifiers, they are noun phrases). Most stand-alone nouns are going to be proper nouns, indefinite pronouns, and plural nouns used with zero articles to make generalizations.

> Gary's **mother** called and asked if Tommy could have dinner at their house.
> It's nobody's **business** but mine!
> Well, it's everybody's **problem** now.
> Children's **games** can get awfully loud.
> A man's **work** is from dawn to setting sun, but a woman's **work** is never done.
>   (traditional saying)
> A retail store's **location** is absolutely critical to its success.
> It will be very expensive to repair all the storm's **damage** quickly.
> Nearly all of the river's **west bank** had been badly eroded by the storm.

Possessive noun phrases

It is important to realize that a possessive noun inside a noun phrase is not just the noun by itself, but also all the words that modify that possessive noun taken as a unit. For example:

My father's sister was born in India.

Think of the phrase *my father* as being a single possessive unit that modifies the head noun *sister*. Inside that unit, *my* modifies *father*. *My* is locked inside its own noun phrase and cannot jump outside its own phrase to modify *sister*. The sister who was born in India was my father's sister, not my sister.

Quantifiers

Quantifiers are determiners that specify the quantity or amount of the noun being modified. Quantifiers are by far the largest and most heterogeneous group of determiners, and they are also the source of most of the mistakes made by both native and nonnative speakers.

The presentation in this chapter is quite different from other chapters in the book. Since there is no accepted classification of quantifiers as there is with determiners, there is also no standard, organized way to talk about quantifiers. Accordingly, we will focus just on the four high-frequency groups of quantifiers that account for the large majority of quantifier errors. Since the errors presented by each of these groups are totally unrelated to the kinds of errors in the other groups, we will deal with each group independently. The four major quantifier errors are (in alphabetical order):

1. *a few / few; a little / little*

2. *a lot of*

3. *all / all (of) the*

4. *many / much*

A *few / few; a little / little*

Few and *little* are used to express small quantities. *Few* is used only with plural count nouns. *Little* is used only with noncount nouns. Using *few* and *little* is greatly complicated by the fact that *few* and *little* each occur in two variant forms with two different meanings: *few* and *a few*, *little* and *a little*. We will discuss *a few / few* first and then turn to *a little / little*.

A *few* and *few*

A few and *few* are quite different in meaning. Compare the following sentences:

a few	Pick up <u>a few</u> loaves of bread on your way home, will you?
few	<u>Few</u> storms in modern times were as damaging as Katrina.

A few is a fixed number expression like *a couple*. *A few* means a small but indefinite quantity. For some people *a few* ranges in meaning from two to six or seven. For other people *a few* has to be at minimum three. (For these people, the meaning of *a few* cannot overlap the meaning of *a couple*—namely two. In other words, for these people *couple* is two and *few* is three or more.) In our example sentence, the person being asked to get *a few* loaves of bread is being asked to get somewhere between two and six or seven loaves of bread. The speaker is leaving the decision of the exact number to the discretion of the person being spoken to.

Few has a quite different meaning from *a few*. According to the dictionary, *few* (as opposed to *a few*) is used to emphasize how small a group of people or things really is. In the sentence,

> <u>Few</u> people around here still remember my grandfather.

few does not mean a quantity between two and six or seven. Using *few* is a way to emphasize or remark on the small number of people who remember the speaker's grandfather.

Let us now turn back to the *few* in our quotation:

> <u>Few</u> storms in modern times were as damaging as Katrina.

Clearly, here *few* is used as a way to emphasize the very small number of storms that were as damaging as Katrina. Equally clearly, *few* does *not* mean "some unspecified but nevertheless real number between two and six or seven."

Another piece of evidence that *a few* and *few* have basically different meanings is that we usually cannot substitute *few* for *a few*. Here is our original example of *a few*:

> Pick up <u>a few</u> loaves of bread on your way home, will you?

When we replace *a few* with *few*, the result is both nonsensical and ungrammatical:

> **X** Pick up <u>few</u> loaves of bread on your way home, will you?

The following are some more sample sentences of both types:

a few
There are still <u>a few</u> parking places on the top deck.
I have <u>a few</u> questions for you if you have time.
Move it <u>a few</u> inches to the left.
I'll get <u>a few</u> bananas for breakfast.
The thermometer has dropped <u>a few</u> degrees in just the last hour.
<u>A few</u> extra rehearsals made all the difference in the world.

few
<u>Few</u> people were aware of how close we came to financial disaster.
There were <u>few</u> people I admired as much as your Aunt Ruth.
<u>Few</u> houses in town are as nice as theirs is.

Few words are as frightening as "There's a problem."
We have had <u>few</u> complaints about the new computer system.
There have been <u>few</u> defects in our new products.

In all of these examples, *a few* means "a small number of," while *few* is used to emphasize the relatively small number of the noun being modified.

Not surprisingly, it is easy to find situations in which *a few* and *few* can have nearly opposite meanings:

a few	We have had <u>a few</u> complaints.
few	We have had <u>few</u> complaints.

The use of *a few* is an acknowledgment that we have indeed had some complaints. In fact, depending on the context, one interpretation of *a few* would be as a euphemism for "we've had a lot of complaints." The use of *few*, of course, is just the opposite. It emphasizes the remarkably small number of complaints there have been, that is, virtually none.

A few and *few* also differ in the way they form questions and negative statements. Compare the following statement and questions:

STATEMENT:	The visitors asked <u>a few</u> questions.
QUESTIONS:	Did the visitors ask <u>a few</u> questions?
	Did the visitors ask <u>any</u> questions?

Both questions are grammatical but semantically different. The version that retains *a few* requires a particular context to make sense. It sounds as if the person asking the question knew in advance that visitors typically do not ask many questions. The question is really asking for conformation of expectations; it is not an actual request for information. However, the version with *any* is a genuine open-ended question that the questioner does not already know the answer to. Here are two more examples:

STATEMENT:	Tom needs to wrap <u>a few</u> presents.
QUESTIONS:	Does Tom need to wrap <u>a few</u> presents?
	Does Tom need to wrap <u>any</u> presents?

The version with *a few* has an expectation of a positive answer. The version with *any* is neutral—the question does not imply an expectation of either a positive or a negative answer.

STATEMENT:	There are <u>a few</u> cars parked in the driveway.
QUESTIONS:	Are there <u>a few</u> cars parked in the driveway?
	Are there <u>any</u> cars parked in the driveway?

The version with *a few* is an odd-sounding question. Since we don't normally expect there to be *any* cars at all parked in a driveway, asking if there are *a few* cars parked there seems almost nonsensical unless the sentence were intended to be ironic: the driveway is actually filled solid with parked cars and the questioner is making a joke about it. The second version with *any* is the only alternative when the context of the question being asked assumes either a yes or no answer. Compare the following statement and questions:

STATEMENT:	Few birds stay here over the winter.
QUESTIONS:	**X** Do few birds stay here over the winter?
	Do any birds stay here over the winter?

The version with *few* is distinctly strange sounding. It is grammatical only if we interpret it as a rhetorical question—a question that the person already knows the answer to and is asking only for confirmation. The second version with *any* is the standard way statements with *few* are turned into questions. In both of the following examples, the question formed with *few* seems strange except as a rhetorical question and the question formed with *any* seems normal:

STATEMENT:	Few students graduate in just four years.
QUESTIONS:	**X** Do few students graduate in just four years?
	Do any students graduate in just four years?

STATEMENT:	Few classes are as hard as this one is.
QUESTIONS:	**X** Are few classes as hard as this one is?
	Are any classes as hard as this one is?

Compare the two different ways of forming negative statements that contain *a few*:

POSITIVE STATEMENT:	There are a few stores here open all night.
NEGATIVE STATEMENTS:	**X** There are not a few stores here open all night.
	There are not any stores here open all night.

The negative statement with *a few* is ungrammatical unless we give an unusually heavy contrastive stress on *not a few* and interpret the sentence as an ironical comment on how many stores are actually open all night. The normal negative form of *a few* is with *any*. For example:

POSITIVE STATEMENT:	John needs a few quarters for the parking meter.
NEGATIVE STATEMENTS:	**X** John does not need a few quarters for the parking meter.
	John does not need any quarters for the parking meter.

POSITIVE STATEMENT:	They got a few maps of the area we are going to.
NEGATIVE STATEMENTS:	**X** They didn't get a few maps of the area we are going to.
	They didn't get any maps of the area we are going to.

Compare the following examples of the negative forms of *a few*:

POSITIVE STATEMENT: <u>Few</u> local newspapers cover world events extensively.

NEGATIVE STATEMENT: <u>Few</u> local papers do not cover world events extensively.

The negative statement is actually grammatical but makes little sense unless the *not* is heavily stressed:

<u>Few</u> local papers do **not** cover world events extensively.

The negative statement makes the assertion that there really are only a few local papers that do **not** cover world events extensively. Negative statements with *few* sound much more normal if we use them in an existential sentence beginning with *there* and put contrastive stress on the negative word:

POSITIVE STATEMENT: There are <u>few</u> federal judges who permit cameras in their courts.

NEGATIVE STATEMENT: There are <u>few</u> federal judges who **don't** permit cameras in their courts.

POSITIVE STATEMENT: There were <u>few</u> questions that the whole class got right.

NEGATIVE STATEMENT: There were <u>few</u> questions that the whole class **didn't** get right.

Few has comparative and superlative forms. We will discuss these in conjunction with the comparative and superlative forms of *little*.

A little and little

A little and *little* are different in meaning. *A little* means "some." *Little* means "none or next to none." (The differences between *a little* and *little* are similar to the differences between *few* and *a few,* but thankfully are much less complicated.) Compare the following sentences:

a little   We have a <u>little</u> money in the budget for your project.
little   We have <u>little</u> money in the budget for your project.

A little means that your project can probably go ahead, but watch your expenses. *Little*, however, means that your project has hardly any chance of being approved.

Here are some more examples along the same lines: *a little* typically means "some, but not a lot"; *little* is usually a euphemism for "virtually none at all."

a little   We have received a <u>little</u> information about the accident. (i.e., some, but not much)
little   We have received <u>little</u> information about the accident. (i.e., we know next to nothing)
a little   The dessert needed a <u>little</u> sugar. (i.e., not sweet enough)
little   The dessert needed <u>little</u> sugar. (i.e., already plenty sweet)
a little   There is a <u>little</u> rain in the forecast. (i.e., some, but not much)
little   There is <u>little</u> rain in the forecast. (i.e., expect the dry weather to continue)

A little and *little* also differ in the way they form questions and negative statements. Compare the following statement and questions:

> STATEMENT: They have a little work to do before dinner.
> QUESTIONS: Do they have a little work to do before dinner?
> Do they have any work to do before dinner?

The question with *a little* is perfectly grammatical, but as we saw with *a few*, *a little* also has a sense of not being a genuine question—we expect the answer to be yes. In fact, many of us would actually change the question with *a little* into a **confirmation question**, a question that asks for confirmation, not actual information. The confirmation question would look like this:

> CONFIRMATION QUESTION: Don't they have a little work to do before dinner?

The implication is that they do know very well they have a ton of work to do. If we wanted to turn the statement with *a little* into a genuine question, we would have to use the version with *any* instead.

The following two more examples show exactly the same kind of difference between *a little* and *any*:

> STATEMENT: They need a little assistance.
> QUESTIONS: Do they need a little assistance?
> Do they need any assistance?
>
> CONFIRMATION QUESTION: Don't they need a little assistance?

With *a little*, there is definitely an expectation that they probably do need some assistance. The use of *any* is much more neutral.

> STATEMENT: The kids have a little dessert after dinner.
> QUESTIONS: Do the kids have a little dessert after dinner?
> Do the kids have any dessert after dinner?
>
> CONFIRMATION QUESTION: Don't the kids have a little dessert after dinner?

The use of *a little* makes the kids' having dessert the normal expectation. *Any* is again much more neutral—the questioner genuinely does not know the family's normal eating practices.

Much as we saw when forming questions with *few*, forming questions with *little* is awkward to the point of being ungrammatical:

> STATEMENT: They have little time for relaxation these days.
> QUESTIONS: X Do they have little time for relaxation these days?
> Do they have any time for relaxation these days?

The first version with *little* can make sense only as an odd kind of rhetorical question. Even then, it is hard imagining a context in which anybody would actually say it. The second version where *any* replaces *little* is much more normal. Here are two more examples with the same difference between questions formed with *little* and questions forms with *any*:

STATEMENT:	I have <u>little</u> butter to spare.
QUESTIONS:	**X** Do you have <u>little</u> butter to spare?
	Do you have <u>any</u> butter to spare?

The question with *little* is again only interpretable as a strange and marginally grammatical rhetorical question. *Any* is perfectly normal.

STATEMENT:	There is <u>little</u> interest in such a risky venture.
QUESTIONS:	Is there <u>little</u> interest in such a risky venture?
	Is there <u>any</u> interest in such a risky venture?

The use of *there* turns the questions with *little* into a grammatical rhetorical question: the questioner is asking only to confirm that there is indeed no interest in the risky venture. It is not a genuine information question the way that the question with *any* is.

Let's review the comparative and superlative forms of *few* and *little*.

BASE	COMPARATIVE	SUPERLATIVE
few	fewer	fewest
little	less	least

few

BASE:	We have had <u>few</u> responses to the new ad.
COMPARATIVE:	We have had <u>fewer</u> responses to the new ad than we would have expected.
SUPERLATIVE:	We have had the <u>fewest</u> responses to the new ad than to any other ad that we have ever used.

little

BASE:	We've had <u>little</u> sunshine this week.
COMPARATIVE:	We've had <u>less</u> sunshine this week than normal.
SUPERLATIVE:	We've had the <u>least</u> sunshine this week than any week this summer.

The comparative forms *fewer* and *less* are the source of a surprising amount of error. The rule seems simple: use *fewer* with count nouns and *less* with noncount nouns. In the earlier examples *fewer* is used with the count noun *responses* and *less* is used with the noncount noun *sunshine*. However, nonnative and native speakers alike unintentionally reverse the rule with surprising frequency and use *fewer* with noncount nouns and *less* with count nouns. The following examples of these errors have the nouns in bold:

fewer used incorrectly with noncount nouns
X We've had <u>fewer</u> **sunshine** this week than normal.
X When both parents are working, they can't help but show <u>fewer</u> **patience** with the kids.
X I don't know about you, but I have a lot <u>fewer</u> **money** than I used to.
X We eat <u>fewer</u> **fruit** when we eat out at fast-food places all the time.

less used incorrectly with count nouns
X We have had <u>less</u> **days** of sunshine than we had last week.
X Everybody made <u>less</u> **mistakes** on their retake of the test.
X Surprisingly, there are <u>less</u> **divorces** in arranged marriages.
X Drivers have <u>less</u> **accidents** on intersections with four-way stops.

Look back at both groups of errors. Which group of errors, *fewer* with noncount nouns or *less* with count nouns, would you have been more likely to have overlooked? The errors go both directions, using *fewer* with noncount nouns and using *less* with count nouns. However, mistakes using *less* with count nouns are much more common than mistakes using *fewer* with noncount nouns.

A lot of

Normally, nouns inside a prepositional phrase do not affect subject-verb agreement. For example, in the following sentence:

The decisions <u>of the committee</u> **are** final. (prepositional phase underlined)

the verb *are* is plural in agreement with the plural noun *decisions*, the subject of the sentence. *Committee*, a singular noun, plays no role in determining subject-verb agreement because it is locked up inside the prepositional phrase *of the committee* and thus cannot affect subject-verb agreement outside the prepositional phrase.

The determiner *a lot of* is highly unusual because the noun that follows the preposition *of* reaches outside the boundaries of its prepositional phrase and preempts the role of the subject so that the following verb agrees with what is actually the *object* of a prepositional phase inside the prepositional phrase. In the following sentences the subject is underlined and the verb is in bold:

A lot of the <u>committee</u> **is** appointed by the board.
A lot of the <u>committees</u> **are** appointed by the board.

As you can see, the verbs *is* and *are* agree with *committee* and *committees* respectively, nouns that are the objects of the preposition *of*. The following three examples have the same structure with the objects of the preposition underlined and the verbs in bold:

> A lot of the <u>team</u> **has** left the field.
> A lot of the <u>teams</u> **have** left the field.
> A lot of the <u>problem</u> **was** caused by poor planning.
> A lot of the <u>problems</u> **were** caused by poor planning.
> A lot of the <u>legal dispute</u> **was** settled out of court.
> A lot of the <u>legal disputes</u> **were** settled out of court.

All / all (of) the

All is used with plural count nouns and noncount nouns:

> PLURAL COUNT: <u>All</u> **repairs** are guaranteed. (plural count noun in bold)
> NONCOUNT: <u>All</u> **luggage** must be stored before takeoff. (noncount noun in bold)

There is one idiomatic use of *all* with contrastive stress that permits *all* to modify singular count nouns:

> I have to read ***all*** of the book by Monday! (*Book* is a singular count noun.)
> I haven't finished ***all*** my program yet! (*Program* is a singular count noun.)
> John took ***all*** the shelf again for his junk! (*Shelf* is a singular count noun.)
> You didn't finish ***all*** the job! (*Job* is a singular count noun.)

These sentences with *all* are usually said in a loud tone of outraged injustice.

All can be combined with definite determiners:

> *All* **those** books go back to the library. (demonstrative determiner)
> *All* **my** children are on their own now. (possessive determiner)

When *all* directly modifies a noun, that noun usually has an unrestricted general meaning. Thomas Jefferson's famous statement in the Declaration of Independence,

> We hold these truths to be evident, that <u>all</u> men are created equal . . .

has an unrestricted universal application for ***all*** people. (Here Jefferson uses *men* in the broad sense of "all mankind," not narrowly as the opposite of *women*.)

All (of) the (as opposed to *all*) usually implies that there is some restriction or limitation (actual or implied) on the group being described. Compare the following sentences:

> UNRESTRICTED: <u>All</u> students must have a pass.
> RESTRICTED: <u>All (of) the</u> students going on the field trip must have a pass.

Using *all (of) the* with an unrestricted generalized noun would be odd:

> **X** *All (of) the* students must have a pass.

This sentence would only be completely appropriate if the sentence were said with extra stress on *all* in response to a challenge about the need for all students to have passes.

> Yes, ***all*** *(of) the* students must have a pass!

Generally the use of *all* and *all of the* are equally grammatical (albeit with the semantic differences described earlier). However, there is one important exception: in negative time expressions *all of the* cannot be used.

all of the	**X** He hasn't been here <u>all of the</u> morning.
all	He hasn't been here <u>all</u> morning.
all of the	**X** We haven't talked to her <u>all of the</u> day.
all	We haven't talked to her <u>all</u> day.
all of the	**X** I haven't seen him <u>all of the</u> week.
all	I haven't seen him <u>all</u> week.
all of the	**X** He hasn't been able to work <u>all of the</u> month.
all	He hasn't been able to work <u>all</u> month.
all of the	**X** The plant hasn't been in operation <u>all of the</u> year.
all	The plant hasn't been in operation <u>all</u> year.

Abstract noncount nouns are often used with *whole* rather than *all (of) the*. Probably the most famous use of *whole* with abstract noncount nouns is in the oath witnesses swear in American courtrooms. The oath says in part that the witness,

> will tell the truth, the <u>whole</u> truth, and nothing but the truth.

Promising to tell "all of the truth" instead of "the whole truth" just doesn't seem adequate. The following examples compare the use of *all* and *whole* with abstract noncount nouns:

> **X** Global warming is threatening <u>all of the</u> environment.
> Global warming is threatening the <u>whole</u> environment.
> **X** <u>All of the</u> issue is getting out of hand.
> The <u>whole</u> issue is getting out of hand.
> **X** <u>All of the</u> experience was quite frightening.
> The <u>whole</u> experience was quite frightening.

As you can see, the preference for *whole* with abstract noncount nouns is not just a mere stylistic preference. Often it is a grammatical requirement.

Many / much

Many and *much* are used to express large quantities. *Many* is used only with plural count nouns. *Much* is used only with noncount nouns. They are very much the counterparts of each other—*many* with count nouns, *much* with noncount nouns. The following are some examples of *many*:

> Many cars and trucks are now manufactured in developing countries.
> I need to hurry; I've got many things to do before I can go home.
> She has many refereed publications in her résumé.
> A large law firm will have many partners.
> That house needs many improvements if they are going to try to sell it.

There is a slight difference in emphasis between *many* and *many of*. Compare the following sentences:

> Many tiles in the bathroom are getting discolored from water stains.
> Many of the tiles in the bathroom are getting discolored from water stains.

Many tiles states that some number of the tiles in the bathroom (more than a few; less than most) have become discolored. *Many of the tiles* implies that a **significant** number of the tiles have become discolored and that something may have to be done about it.

Much is used only with noncount nouns:

> There has been much debate about the value of the Internet.
> The class hasn't shown much improvement.
> Young kids have too much homework these days.
> There is not much air here at the top of the mountains.
> How much coffee should we make?
> Much work remains to be done.

Much is often used in questions and negative statements—more so than its counterpart *many*. The difference in usage probably reflects how hard it is to use noncount nouns in statements. The statement,

> Much luggage is left.

is grammatical but stilted. However, the question and negative forms of the same sentence seem perfectly normal:

> Is much luggage left?
> Not much luggage is left.

For a similar reason we probably use *much of the* more frequently than *many of the*. Compare the following sentences:

> We have already done *much* work.
> We have already done *much of the* work.

There really is little if any difference in meaning between the two sentences, but the one with *much of the* sounds normal and the sentence with just *much* sounds quite odd.

Another way we avoid the awkwardness of *much* in statements is to substitute a quantity phrase with *of* instead of *much*. So rather than saying,

> There has been <u>much</u> debate about the project.

we might use the following quantity phrases:

> There has been <u>a lot of</u> debate about the project.
> There has been <u>plenty of</u> debate about the project.
> There has been <u>lots of</u> debate about the project.
> There has been <u>a great deal of</u> debate about the project.

It is quite common to alternate between *much* in negative statements and questions with using quantity phrases in affirmative statements:

NEGATIVE:	We don't have <u>much</u> time.
QUESTION:	How <u>much</u> time do we have?
STATEMENT:	We have <u>a lot of</u> time. (quantity phrase)
NEGATIVE:	I don't have <u>much</u> homework to do tonight.
QUESTION:	How <u>much</u> homework do you have to do tonight?
STATEMENT:	I have <u>lots of</u> homework to do tonight. (quantity phrase)

Much and *many* are among the few determiners that have comparative and superlative forms:

BASE	COMPARATIVE	SUPERLATIVE
much	more	most
many	more	most

much

BASE:	There was <u>much</u> unhappiness about the judge's decision.
COMPARATIVE:	There was even <u>more</u> unhappiness after the results were announced.
SUPERLATIVE:	But the <u>most</u> unhappiness resulted from the court's refusal to address the issue of corruption.

many

BASE:	There are <u>many</u> accidents at that intersection.
COMPARATIVE:	There are <u>more</u> accidents there than anywhere else in the city.
SUPERLATIVE:	The <u>most</u> accidents take place at the southeast corner.

Review of quantifiers

This section contains a number of short exercises, one for each of the main topics covered in this chapter of the book. The exercises serve both as a review and as a way for you to test your own understanding of the various topics presented in this section.

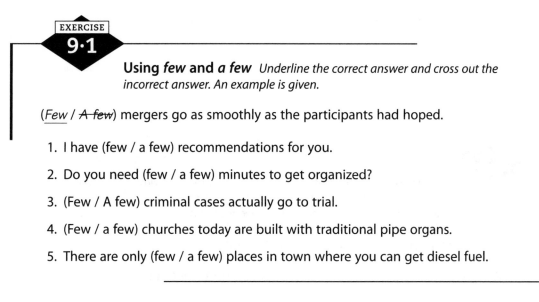

EXERCISE 9·1

Using *few* and *a few* *Underline the correct answer and cross out the incorrect answer. An example is given.*

(*Few* / ~~A few~~) mergers go as smoothly as the participants had hoped.

1. I have (few / a few) recommendations for you.

2. Do you need (few / a few) minutes to get organized?

3. (Few / A few) criminal cases actually go to trial.

4. (Few / a few) churches today are built with traditional pipe organs.

5. There are only (few / a few) places in town where you can get diesel fuel.

EXERCISE 9·2

Questions with *few* and *a few* *Turn the following statements with* few *and* a few *into corresponding question forms. Assume that all questions are genuine requests for information (as opposed to requests for confirmation). An example is given.*

Few houses in California have basements.

Do _any_ *houses in California have basements?*

1. Few states charge sales taxes on basic food items.

   _____

2. The kids got a few mosquito bites in the park.

   _____

3. <u>Few</u> children could sit still through such a long performance.

_____

4. <u>Few</u> eyewitness statements are completely accurate.

_____

5. There are <u>a few</u> seats available for tonight's performance.

_____

The meaning of _little_ and _a little_ _Each of the following sentences is followed by the intended meaning of_ little _or_ a little _in that sentence. Select the quantifier that best expresses the intended meaning. Show your choice by underlining either_ little _or_ a little _as appropriate and crossing out the inappropriate alternative. An example is given._

There was (little / a little) resistance to the proposal. (some, but not a lot)

There was (~~little~~ / <u>a little</u>) resistance to the proposal.

1. The students showed (little / a little) enthusiasm for the project. (hardly any at all)

_____

2. The flood caused (little / a little) damage to our property. (some, but not a lot)

_____

3. (Little / A little) progress was reported in the negotiations. (hardly any at all)

_____

4. (Little / A little) smoke was leaking out from the fireplace. (some, but not a lot)

_____

5. (Little / A little) thought had gone into the design. (hardly any at all)

_____

Subject-verb agreement with *a lot of* Determine whether the singular or plural form of the verb in parentheses correctly agrees with the subject. Underline the correct form and cross out the incorrect form. An example is given.

A lot of accidents (is / are) caused by diver inattention.

A lot of accidents (is / are) caused by diver inattention.

1. A lot of windows (was / were) damaged in the storm.

   _____

2. A lot of our concern (was / were) totally unjustified.

   _____

3. A lot of the luggage on our flight (was / were) delayed.

   _____

4. Fortunately, a lot of the injuries in the accident (was / were) relatively minor.

   _____

5. A lot of advice you get (is / are) well-intended, but not all that helpful.

   _____

Choosing between *all* and *all of the* If the phrase in italics is correct, write OK. If it is not, indicate that the sentence is ungrammatical and cross out the incorrect phrase. Then supply the correct form. An example is given.

I didn't have a minute to myself *all of the* day.

X *I didn't have a minute to myself all of the day.*

I didn't have a minute to myself all *day.*

1. We didn't have any heat *all of the* weekend.

_____

2. *All of the* players were ready for a break.

_____

3. It seems like I have spent *all of the* day waiting on hold for customer service.

_____

4. Did you finish *all of the* exercises before class?

_____

5. We have to call a plumber. The faucet in the kitchen leaked *all of the* night.

_____

Using *much* and *many* Underline the correct form, and cross out the incorrect form. An example is given.

We need to explore (much / many) options before we make a final decision.

We need to explore (~~much~~ / many) options before we make a final decision.

1. (Much / Many) merchants are reluctant to accept credit cards for small purchases.

_____

2. There was way too (much / many) discussion and not nearly enough action.

_____

3. We didn't get (much / many) support from the home office.

_____

4. (Much / Many) injuries required hospitalization.

_____

5. Was there (much / many) participation by the newer students?

_____

Answer key

 ARTICLES

1 An introduction to articles

1·1
1. ∅ (zero) Family names come from all over the (def.) world.
2. An (sing. indef.) interest payment will be due on the (def.) first of the (def.) month.
3. What they did really took some (indef. some) courage.
4. ∅ (zero) Players have to enter the (def.) stadium though a (sing. indef.) special gate.
5. Some (indef. *some*) costs cannot be passed on to ∅ (zero) customers and must be absorbed by the (def.) company.
6. ∅ (zero) Experience is a (sing. indef.) stern and unforgiving teacher.
7. They inherited ∅ (zero) property on the (def.) coast from a (sing. indef.) distant relative.
8. The (def.) police were not able to find any (indef. *some*) solid evidence connecting the (def.) initial suspects to the (def.) crime.
9. Technically, ∅ (zero) glass is not a (sing. indef.) solid, because it does not have a (sing. indef.) rigid structure.
10. Some (indef. *some*) fish is very high in ∅ (zero) omega-e fatty acid.

1·2
1. I made a (sing. indef.) big mistake (sing. count) right at the (def.) beginning. (sing. count)
2. We are really trying to cut back on ∅ (zero) salt. (noncount)
3. Some (indef. *some*) versions (pl. count) of the (def.) story (sing. count) have a (sing. indef.) totally different outcome. (sing. count)
4. ∅ (zero) Big projects (pl. count) always tend to run out of ∅ (zero) time. (noncount)
5. The (def.) team (sing. count) has shown some (indef. *some*) signs (pl. count) of ∅ (zero) improvement (noncount) lately.
6. We got a (sing. indef.) loan (sing. count) to make some (indef. *some*) repairs. (pl. count)
7. He deals with the (def.) integration (noncount) of different computer ∅ (zero) systems. (pl. count)
8. The (def.) failures (pl. count) came as a (sing. indef.) complete surprise. (sing. count)
9. ∅ (zero) People (pl. count) are too busy these days.
10. The (def.) university (sing. count) offers a (sing. indef.) number (sing. count) of ∅ (zero) scholarships. (pl. count)

1·3
1. noncount mass
2. count

3. noncount mass
4. count
5. count
6. noncount mass
7. count
8. noncount mass
9. count
10. count

A probable answer: Any object that you can easily pick up in your fingers is probably a count noun. Any object that you cannot easily pick up in your fingers is probably a mass noun.

1·4
1. ungrammatical because *honey* is a noncount noun—the name of a liquid
2. ungrammatical because *gases* is a noncount noun—the name of a gas
3. ungrammatical because *seawater* is a noncount noun—the name of a liquid
4. grammatical because *streams* is a plural count noun
5. ungrammatical because *haze* is a noncount noun—the name of a gas
6. grammatical because *some lemonades* is a contracted form of a prepositional phrase containing *of*: *some bottles/glasses of lemonade*
7. grammatical because *eggs* is a plural count noun
8. ungrammatical because *lemonade* is a noncount noun—the name of a liquid
9. ungrammatical because *exhausts* is a noncount noun—the name of a gas
10. ungrammatical because *batter* is a noncount noun—the name of a liquid

1·5
1. quarters, dimes, dollars, pennies, **X** monies
2. **X** fruits, apples, bananas, peaches, oranges
3. wrappers, scraps, banana peels, **X** trashes, cartons
4. cars, buses, **X** traffics, trucks, motorcycles
5. **X** silverwares, knives, forks, spoons
6. staplers, computers, copiers, printers, **X** equipments
7. mountains, **X** sceneries, lakes, waterfalls, valleys
8. shoes, boots, sandals, heels, **X** footwears
9. apartments, flats, houses, **X** housings, rooms
10. facts, opinions, **X** informations, notes, memos, lists

1·6
1. (b) activity
2. (c) natural phenomena
3. (b) activity
4. (c) natural phenomena
5. (b) activity
6. (a) derived noun ending in *-ness*
7. (b) activity
8. (c) natural phenomena
9. (b) activity
10. (a) derived noun ending in *-ness*

2 The definite article *the*

2·1

	ðə/	ðiy/
1. umbrella		X
2. desk	X	
3. name	X	
4. insurance		X
5. eraser		X
6. test	X	
7. road	X	
8. action		X
9. building	X	
10. organization		X

2·2

	/ðə/	/ðiy/
1. unicorn		X
2. honor		X
3. happiness	X	
4. ultimate		X
5. horror	X	
6. humble	X	
7. utensils		X
8. upset	X	
9. hunger	X	
10. honest		X

2·3

1. /ðə/
2. /ðiy/
3. /ðə/
4. /ðiy/
5. /ðə/
6. /ðiy/
7. /ðiy/
8. /ðə/
9. /ðə/
10. /ðiy/

2·4

1. **The** Air Force Academy is located in ∅ Colorado Springs.
2. A snow storm in **the** Cascades has closed ∅ Highway I-90.
3. **The** Washington Monument is the tallest structure in ∅ Washington, DC.
4. **The** Dr. Brown whom I was talking about is our dentist.
5. The company is replacing **the** treasurer in ∅ July.
6. **The** Faroe Islands are off the coast of ∅ Norway.
7. ∅ Easter is unusually early this year.
8. **The** Sacramento is the longest river in ∅ California.

9. The English novelist ∅ G. K. Chesterton wrote many mystery stories featuring ∅ <u>Father Brown</u>.
10. <u>**The** Christmas I was talking about must have been when we were still living on</u> ∅ <u>Ellsworth Street</u>. (Note: we use *the* with *Christmas* because *Christmas* is followed by a post-noun modifier. Normally *the* would not be used with *Christmas*.)

2·5
1. (b) defined by modifiers
2. (c) normal expectations (We expect houses to have kitchens.)
3. (a) previous mention
4. (b) defined by modifiers
5. (d) uniqueness
6. (c) normal expectations (We expect office buildings to have elevators and top floors.)
7. (b) defined by modifiers
8. (a) previous mention
9. (c) normal expectations (We expect books to have tables of contents.)
10. (b) defined by modifiers

3 The singular indefinite article *a/an*

3·1
1. an, a
2. an
3. an, an
4. an
5. An, a
6. a
7. An, an
8. an
9. an
10. an, a

3·2
1. (b) introduce nonspecific new topic
2. (c) characterize or define
3. (a) introduce specific new topic
4. (d) make generalizations
5. (a) introduce specific new topic
6. (b) introduce nonspecific new topic or (d) make generalizations
7. (a) introduce specific new topic
8. (d) make generalizations
9. (c) characterize or define
10. (b) introduce nonspecific new topic

4 The indefinite article *some*

4·1
1. any
2. some
3. any
4. some

5. any
6. any
7. any
8. some
9. any
10. any

4·2
1. OK
2. any
3. any
4. OK
5. any
6. any
7. OK
8. any
9. any
10. any

4·3
1. (b) *some/any* adverbial *before* clause rule
2. (b) *some/any* adverbial *before* clause rule
3. (c) *some/any too* predicate adjective rule
4. (c) *some/any too* predicate adjective rule
5. (a) *some/any* adverbial *if* clause rule
6. (a) *some/any* adverbial *if* clause rule
7. (a) *some/any* adverbial *if* clause rule
8. (c) *some/any too* predicate adjective rule
9. (c) *some/any too* predicate adjective rule
10. (b) *some/any* adverbial *before* clause rule

5 The zero article

5·1
1. ∅
2. ∅
3. the
4. ∅
5. ∅
6. ∅
7. The, the
8. ∅, an
9. the, the
10. ∅, a, ∅
11. ∅
12. ∅
13. ∅, ∅
14. the, ∅, ∅
15. ∅, a

5·2 ∅ Travel by ∅ air has become everyone's favorite topic to complain about. We all have heard ∅ stories about ∅ passengers being stuck for hours on ∅ runways and ∅ stories about ∅ endless lines at ∅ ticket counters. These are all true. The problem is that none of us is willing to pay what it would cost to fix the problems. None of us wants to pay a penny more than we have to. When ∅ airlines try to raise ∅ prices to improve their services, we all go to the airlines that have not raised their prices. When ∅ airports try to get approval to raise ∅ taxes to pay for ∅ airport improvements, we vote the bond issues down.

II ◆ DETERMINERS

7 An introduction to determiners

7·1
1. true adjective
2. determiner
3. determiner
4. true adjective
5. determiner
6. true adjective
7. determiner, true adjective
8. determiner
9. true adjective
10. true adjective, determiner

7·2
1. unexpected—true adjective: comparative: more unexpected; superlative: most unexpected
2. double—determiner: comparative: **X** more double; superlative: **X** most double
3. last—determiner: comparative: **X** last-er; superlative: **X** last-est
4. rapid—true adjective: comparative: more rapid; superlative: most rapid
5. neither—determiner: comparative: **X** more neither; superlative: **X** most neither
6. enthusiastic—true adjective: comparative: more enthusiastic; superlative: most enthusiastic
7. That—determiner: comparative: **X** that-er; superlative: that-est
8. dirty—true adjective: comparative: dirtier; superlative: dirtiest
9. amazing—true adjective: comparative: more amazing; superlative: most amazing
10. enough—determiner: comparative: **X** more enough; superlative: **X** most enough

7·3
1. It is hard when both are out of school at the same time.
2. Take whichever you want.
3. Each seems worse than the previous one.
4. The audience will have a few to ask the speaker.
5. They will probably accept whatever you give them.
6. We couldn't decide which we wanted to see.
7. Unfortunately, we had little to spare.
8. The first always seems to stick to the pan.
9. Most go to public schools.
10. This is never going to work.

7·4
1. After a few false starts, I finally got the right answer.
2. The detective noticed numerous parallel scars on the victim's face.
3. Those woolen blankets need to be cleaned.
4. The patient was taking many shallow breaths.
5. Most urban landscapes need more green space.
6. Few beginning jobs pay a very good wage.
7. Such a poor outcome should have been anticipated.
8. My best guess turned out to be far too low.
9. We looked at several comparable houses over the weekend.
10. Their program has produced dozens of local physicians.

8   Definite determiners

8·1
1. Expansion test: OK I'm afraid that it is a problem we have no easy solution for.
2. Expansion test: **X** Like many older cities, it is downtown has suffered extensive decay.
                                   its
3. Expansion test: **X** After the bankruptcy, it is assets were frozen by the court.
4. Expansion test: OK It is a solution in search of a problem.
                    its
5. Expansion test: **X** I must say, it is architecture came as an absolute surprise.
                         its
6. Expansion test: **X** Fortunately, it is limitations are well known.
                       its
7. Expansion test: **X** The movie was very affecting; it is final scenes were really moving.
8. Expansion test: OK It is a controversy that never seems to end.
                   its
9. Expansion test: **X** We have been discussing it is surprising success.
                       its
10. Expansion test: **X** The facility has totally outgrown it is maximum capacity.
                        its

9   Quantifiers

9·1
1. I have (~~few~~ / a few) recommendations for you.
2. Do you need (~~few~~ / a few) minutes to get organized?
3. (Few / ~~A few~~) criminal cases actually go to trial.
4. (Few / ~~a few~~) churches today are built with traditional pipe organs.
5. There are only (~~few~~ / a few) places in town where you can get diesel fuel.

9·2
1. Do any states charge sales taxes on basic food items?
2. Did the kids get any mosquito bites in the park?
3. Could any children sit still through such a long performance?
4. Are any eyewitness statements completely accurate?
5. Are any seats available for tonight's performance?

9·3
1. The students showed (little / ~~a little~~) enthusiasm for the project. (hardly any at all)
2. The flood caused (~~little~~ / a little) damage to our property. (some, but not a lot)
3. (Little / ~~A little~~) progress was reported in the negotiations. (hardly any at all)
4. (~~Little~~ / A little) smoke was leaking out from the fireplace. (some, but not a lot)
5. (Little / ~~A little~~) thought had gone into the design. (hardly any at all)

9·4
1. A lot of windows (~~was~~ / were) damaged in the storm.
2. A lot of our concern (was / ~~were~~) totally unjustified.
3. A lot of the luggage on our flight (was / ~~were~~) delayed.
4. Fortunately, a lot of the injuries in the accident (~~was~~ / were) relatively minor.
5. A lot of advice you get (is / ~~are~~) well-intended, but not all that helpful.

9·5
1. **X** We didn't have any heat ~~all of the~~ weekend.
   We didn't have any heat *all* weekend.
2. OK
3. It seems like I have spent ~~all of the~~ day waiting on hold for customer service.
   It seems like I have spent *all* day waiting on hold for customer service.
4. OK
5. The faucet in the kitchen leaked ~~all of the~~ night.
   The faucet in the kitchen leaked *all* night.

9·6
1. (~~Much~~ / Many) merchants are reluctant to accept credit cards for small purchases.
2. There was way too (much / ~~many~~) discussion and not nearly enough action.
3. We didn't get (much / ~~many~~) support from the home office.
4. (~~Much~~ / Many) injuries required hospitalization.
5. Was there (much / ~~many~~) participation by the newer students?